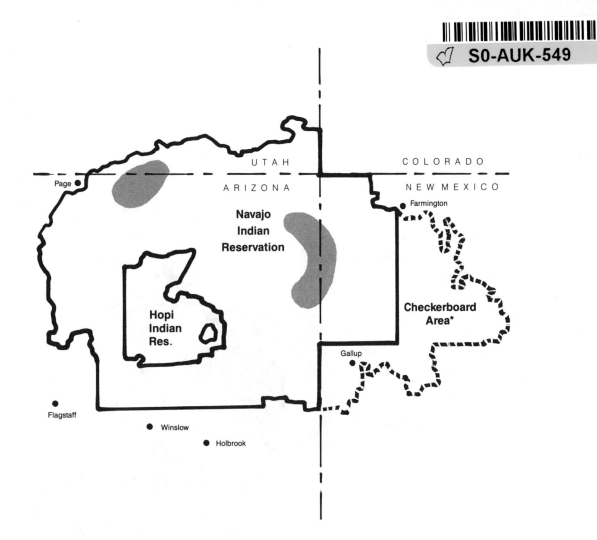

UTAH

COLORADO

Page

ARIZONA

NEW MEXICO

Farmington

Navajo
Indian
Reservation

Hopi
Indian
Res.

Checkerboard
Area*

Gallup

Flagstaff

Winslow

Holbrook

The plants described in Nanise' grow on the Navajo Reservation, a 25,209-square-mile area covering the northeastern corner of Arizona, the northwestern corner of New Mexico, and a portion of southeastern Utah. The area is comparable in size to the state of West Virginia.

 Elevations above 7,000 feet

*Checkerboard Area, Mixed Lands (State, BLM, Navajo)

Whipple cholla
(*Opuntia whipplei*)

NANISE' *A Navajo Herbal*

One Hundred Plants from the Navajo Reservation

by VERNON O. MAYES
and BARBARA BAYLESS LACY

with Illustrations by JACK AHASTEEN
and JASON CHEE

Barbara Lacy
12/96.

Here's To plants
our lifes depends
on theirs

Navajo Community College Press
Tsaile, Arizona 1989

Dedicated
to our parents
Verner Ogle and Ethel Woods Mayes
and
Al and Margaret Lynch Bayless
and
The Lacy Family

This publication was initiated
pursuant to Division of Health, Education
and Welfare Contract No. HRA-232-29-002.

Library of Congress Catalog Card Number 85-62613
International Standard Book Number 0-912586-62-1

The drawing on page 143 of the Woman with Cradle, from "An Ethnologic
Dictionary of the Navajo Language," 1910, is used with the permission of the
Franciscan Fathers, St. Michaels, Arizona.

CONTENTS

MAGGIE DAWES, Navajo herbalist from Fuzzy Mountain, shows visitors some of the medicinal herbs that grow in her area.

PREFACE

In 1972, the Navajo Tribal Council chartered the Navajo Health Authority to research, plan, and develop programs that would improve the health and well being of the Navajo people. One of the Navajo Health Authority's charges was to integrate traditional and western medicine on the reservation.

The Navajo Ethnobotany Project was established to collect previously published Navajo ethnobotanical information and make it available to the Navajo people. It had a twofold goal: to awaken students' interest in Navajo culture as well as in the possibility of science careers.

Navajo plant uses have been transcribed since explorers, missionaries, traders, and soldiers first encountered the Navajo people. Their reports, and those of early scientists, were published in limited scholarly editions, often left in university libraries if distributed at all, and thus seldom available to the Navajo people.

The manuscripts were written by people who often knew anthropology but not botany as well as by people who knew neither. Some spoke Navajo, others didn't. Yet the manuscripts from across the decades and miles have a similarity that can only testify to the extensive knowledge and use of plants among the Navajo.

Nanise' is a compilation of some of the information in those manuscripts. No new information was collected in deference to those who believe the Navajo's plant knowledge is sacred and should not be made public. We have added drawings, photos, plant descriptions, and growing areas to help the reader identify each plant.

Nanise' was limited to 100 of the plants the Navajos used in everyday life. A few plants with no apparent uses were included because they illustrate the Navajos' belief that the plants within the four sacred mountains were gifts from the Holy People. Recently introduced plants have no traditional uses.

Nanise' should be read as a testament to the Navajos' knowledge, not as a pharmacopaeia. The medicinal and ceremonial information is purposely brief. Only Navajos who have gone through an extensive apprenticeship with a medicine-person should have access to medicinal and ceremonial information.

The botanical descriptions apply specifically to the

reservation plant species and thus, may not encompass the species generally.

Voucher specimens, collected by one author since 1958, are distributed at the Navajo Community College herbarium, two hundred specimens; the Northern Arizona University herbarium, one hundred specimens; the College of Ganado herbarium, one hundred specimens; and the collection of Vernon Mayes, one thousand specimens.

The plant descriptions and plant habitats were written from field notes (observations, informants' comments, surveys of vegetation) as well as from herbarium sheets. Field observations include measurements of live plants, altimeter readings of plant communities, step-point transects, and conversations with Navajos in the area.

We want to thank the many people who helped put this book together. It started with Dr. Alan Goodman, director of the Navajo Health Authority who was the first to say, Write a book, and the Navajo Health Authority Board of Commissioners, who gave their approval. Others include Lloyd Thompson, Jack Jackson, Eddie Tso, and the rest of the NHA staff; and Garnet and Francis Draper; reviewers Dr. S. Ross Tocher, University of Michigan, and Dr. J. M. Rominger, Northern Arizona University; Wendy Hodgson and Bruce Parfitt, Desert Botanical Garden, Phoenix, Arizona; and Dr. William Martin, University of New Mexico.

INTRODUCTION

THE LAND

The land is beautiful. The Navajo Reservation's stark and startling sandstone formations have been used as the backdrop for motion pictures, tourist brochures, and advertisements. The painted desert is seen in all directions, and in untraveled areas petrified wood lies undisturbed. The land ranges from a surrealist desert, where NASA tested moon-landing equipment in the 1960s, to tall pine forests surrounding sparkling trout-filled lakes.

The 25,209-square-mile Navajo Reservation covers the northeast corner of Arizona, the northwest corner of New Mexico, and tips into Utah. Most of the land is semiarid, high, plateau country. It has two mountain ranges, deep canyons, low-lying plains, and high deserts. Thirty-five percent of the area is steppe (vast semiarid plains like those found in southeast Europe and Siberia), and 8 percent is forest. Mixed among this are over 1,500,000 acres of badlands such as canyons and mesas.

The land is harsh. High temperatures during the summer and subzero temperatures during winter, high winds, and frequent dust storms are characteristic. Droughts periodically occur, and frosts have been recorded in every month of the year.

The land is dry. Annual rainfall varies from 27 inches at high elevations to 6 inches at low elevations. Half of the area averages 8 inches a year.

But being Navajo is inextricably related to this land between the Navajo sacred mountains: Blanca Peak in the east, Mount Taylor in the south, the San Francisco Peaks in the west, and Mount Hesperus in the north. The Holy People gave the Navajos the land between the four sacred mountains and they thrived.

The Navajos were in the Southwest before A.D. 1500. Their oral tradition says that they arrived from four underworlds. When they arrived in this world, they became the *Diné,* the people known today as the Navajos. They were a self-sufficient and religious people who needed nothing other than the resources of their land to survive.

A major change in their life occurred when they acquired sheep from the Spanish in the 1500s. Since then the Navajos have been a pastoral people whose lives follow the rhythms of their livestock.

Major changes are again occurring on the Navajo Reservation as the Navajo join the quickening pace of modern life. Yet, plant use continues; it is part of the religion and fabric of life of the Navajo people. Plants are respected as a perpetually renewing gift of the Holy People.

PLANT USE

Wild plants are gathered for food, for medicine, and for religion, in the everyday life of the Navajo people. The plant uses are prescribed by centuries-old rituals, by a belief in the oneness of creation, and by a reverence for all living things. The rules for living began in the creation stories of the Navajo people. The stories not only explain how and why animals and plants were created, but how they relate to the Diné, the Navajo people. Yucca is a good example.

In the days when monsters ruled the earth, the gods watched one particularly troublesome bad bear-monster. Finally, they told him, "Since you have been so destructive to the Navajo people, you will evermore provide them with food, clothing, and soap."

The bear was destroyed and where pieces of the bear landed, a yucca grew. Navajos once made fiber ropes and shoes from yucca, and today yucca is used for ceremonial items. The fruit is considered a delicacy and as everyone knows, yucca suds make the best shampoo.

Almost every detail of Navajo life was first mentioned in the creation stories. Even games.

When the world was created, the gods could not decide how to divide day and night. Some gods wanted the world to be continuously light; others wanted it to be dark. They decided the only fair way to make a decision was by playing a game. The winners would decide if the world was to be light or dark. The Moccasin Game was born.

The people divided themselves into two teams, animals and birds. Of course, every area of the reservation has developed its own variation of the game, but basically it is played today by the same rules as were handed down in the creation stories.

Two teams are chosen, one black, one gray. One person acts as an official. Pits are dug on the north and south sides of the hogan or playing field. Four moccasins are placed in each pit. A disc (about the size of a quarter, blackened on one side made from the base of an ear of corn) is dropped from waist height by the official. (The team of the person who blackens the disc is automatically the "blacks.") The team that wins the disc drop is the first to hide the turquoise. Holding a blanket in front of them, they hide the turquoise in the toe of one of the moccasins. The other side must guess where the stone is. As the game is played, 102 songs associated with the game are sung. Score is kept with 102 yucca leaf counters (about 6 inches long). Points are awarded by the number of guesses it takes to find the turquoise: 10, 6, or 4 points are awarded accordingly. The game ends when all counters are held by one side.

But before the game starts, a turquoise offering is made to the yucca plant that furnished the counters. A final offering (usually a turquoise) is made with a prayer at the end of the game, and the counters and other game equipment are buried at that time.

New games, modern pots, pans, and other household items, grocery store food, and western medicine have changed the Navajos' dependence on plants. But traditional ways in religion, in medicine, in behavior are still valued elements of Navajo life today.

Certain games must be played, ceremonies held, and foods for special occasions, weaving implements and the loom must be made as they always have been, or not done or made at all. Navajos who know how to do things "the Navajo way" are respected for that knowledge.

Prayer accompanies all plant use on the Navajo Reservation. Prayers are said when Rocky Mountain bee plant

(Cleome serrulata) is gathered for stew, when yarrow *(Achillea lanulosa)* is picked to cure a skin disease, when a sacred plant is gathered to treat a horse's sore leg, when a variety of plants are picked to make a rainbow of soft, long-lasting wool dyes.

Plants are not picked randomly or wastefully. Rather, they are picked as needed, and then, no more than are necessary.

An herbalist finds two of a particular species that she wishes to pick. To the largest and healthiest plant, she says a prayer and explains why she must pick its neighbor. An offering of shell, pollen, or other sacred material is deposited with the first plant. Then she picks what she needs. Afterward, the plant remains are buried with a final prayer.

For more information on *Nanise',* we hope you will contact a Navajo medicineman or herbalist. Over seven hundred Hataalii are practicing on the Navajo Reservation today. They are the experts on Navajo herbs. We ask that you observe their laws.

Finally, who won the first Moccasin Game? It was a tie. That's why we have both day and night.

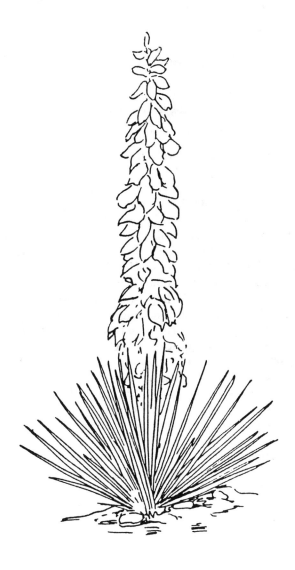

Soapweed *(Yucca angustissima)*

3

ALDER *(Alnus)*
thinleaf alder, black alder

Alnus incana (L.) Moench ('al-nuss in-'kay-nuh)
Alnus: From alders, an old English word, *alor,* with a
    phonetic "d" added
incana: Grayish white, hoary

NAVAJO NAME: *K'ish,* "alder"

DESCRIPTION & DISTRIBUTION

Thinleaf alder may be a deciduous shrub or a small tree as
tall as 12 feet. Twigs are purplish brown; old bark is red-
brown to gray-brown. Leaf blades are coarsely and finely
toothed and may reach 3 inches in length. Female catkins
(drooping flower clusters) harden and darken to become
small conelike structures approximately ½ inch long. This
alder resembles water birch *(Betula occidentalis),* but the latter
lacks "cones," has single-toothed leaves, and reddish brown
younger bark with lenticels (prominent marks or bumps).

    Thinleaf alder is scattered along streams in mountains
and narrow canyons of Navajoland between elevations of
6,000 and 8,500 feet in forests of Gambel oak *(Quercus
gambelii)* and Rocky Mountain juniper *(Juniperus
scopulorum),* and of Douglas fir *(Pseudotsuga menziesii)* and
Colorado blue spruce *(Picea pungens).* Associates are water
birch *(Betula occidentalis),* Gambel oak *(Quercus gambelii),*
gooseberries *(Ribes* sp.*),* and inland box elder *(Acer negundo).*

NAVAJO USES

HOUSEHOLD: *K'ish* was used to make spears, and dyes for
wool, leather, and basketry. To make the spear, a 7- or
8-foot alder branch, about 3 inches in diameter, was
pounded with stones to harden it. After it was approximately half as big, it was decorated with a tuft of eagle
feathers.

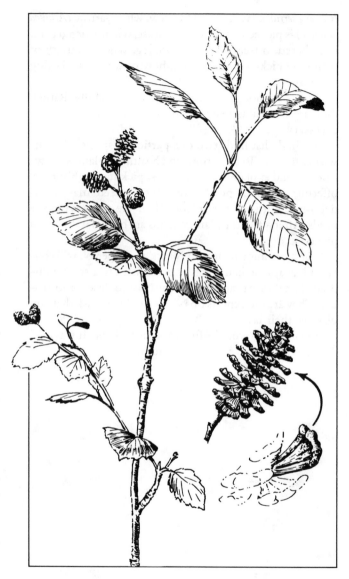

Red, tan, and brown dyes are made from alder bark. The red, all-vegetable, wool dye is made from juniper (*Juniperus occidentalis*), mountain mahogany (*Cercocarpus montanus*), alder, and an unidentified moss. Roots of mountain mahogany are crushed and boiled. Juniper twig ashes, powdered alder bark, and a lichen called *ni'hadlaad*, which acts as a mordant, are added. The dye is boiled and strained; wool is soaked overnight.

A dull reddish wool dye and a tan buckskin dye are made of powdered alder bark and mountain mahogany rootbark. A red leather dye is made of juniper root and mountain mahogany. These are crushed and boiled. Pulverized alder bark and juniper ashes are added, and the dye is reboiled. The dye is applied warm to one or both sides of leather. A pale red basketry dye is made by boiling juniper root and mountain mahogany together before adding ground alder bark. Juniper ashes are added to enhance the color of the dye. See appendix, page 139 for light brown dye recipe.

REFERENCES

Elmore, Francis, *Ethnobotany of the Navajo*, 39.
Franciscan Fathers, *An Ethnologic Dictionary of the Navajo Language*, 188, 232–33, 293, 296, 304, 316.
Kluckhohn, Clyde, et al., *Navajo Material Culture*, 364–65.
Martin, Neils, *Common Range Plants*, 1.
Young, Stella, *Native Plants Used by the Navajo*, 37, 46, 56–58.

ALKALI PINK (*Sphaeralcea*)
scarlet false-mallow, red globe-mallow

Sphaeralcea coccinea (Pursh) Rydb. (sfeer-'ral-see-uh kok-'sin-ee-uh)
Sphaeralcea: From the Greek *sphaira*, "globe," because the seeds are in globular heads, and *alcea*, "mallow"
coccinea: From the Latin *coccinus*, "scarlet," which comes from an earlier Greek word for "berry," *kokkos*

NAVAJO NAME: *Azee' ntl'iní*, "gummy medicine"

DESCRIPTION & DISTRIBUTION

Scarlet false-mallow is a short (usually under 1 foot), perennial globe-mallow with medium-sized, reddish flowers and deeply cut leaves. The fruit is shaped like a concave button with several parts that eventually separate. Stems and leaves have small, asterisk-like, branched hairs. Flowers April through August.

Scattered patches of scarlet false-mallow occur at elevations of about 5,000 feet to about 7,000 feet in communities of shadscale (*Atriplex confertifolia*) and black greasewood (*Sarcobatus vermiculatus*), big sagebrush (*Artemisia tridentata*) and fourwing saltbush (*Atriplex canescens*), and Colorado pinyon (*Pinus edulis*) and junipers (*Juniperus* sp.) on medium to fine soils. Other globe-mallows (*Sphaeralcea* sp.), dropseeds (*Sporobolus* sp.), knotweeds (*Polygonum* sp.), goosefoots (*Chenopodium* sp.), and pigweeds (*Amaranthus* sp.) are associates in swales and along roadsides.

NAVAJO USES

MEDICINAL: This plant's Navajo name came from the sticky mixture that occurs when the roots and leaves are pounded and soaked in water. The resulting sticky infusion is put on sores to stop bleeding and is used as a lotion for skin disease.

The dried powdered plant is used as dusting powder.

5

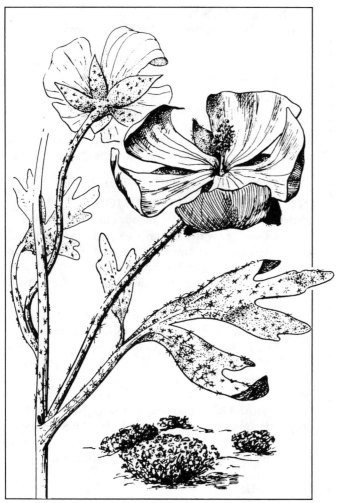

Scarlet false-mallow is one of the life medicines, (see yarrow); it is used as a tonic to improve the appetite, and to cure colds, coughs, and flu.

CEREMONIAL: Medicine men drink *azee' ntł'iní* for strength. It is also a principal Coyote Way, Beauty Way, and Night Way medicine.

OTHER: The top of the plant can be made into a beverage or dried for tobacco.

Azee' ntł'iní was said to have been eaten in times of food shortages. It has little food value for animals.

Scarlet false-mallow is a poor soil binder and it is not an effective plant in areas undergoing erosion.

REFERENCES

Elmore, Francis, *Ethnobotany of the Navajo*, 63.

Franciscan Fathers, *An Ethnologic Dictionary of the Navajo Language*, 115, 194.

Hocking, George M., "Some Plant Materials Used Medicinally and Otherwise by the Navaho Indians in the Chaco Canyon, New Mexico," *El Palacio*, 161–62.

Matthews, Washington, "Navajo Names for Plants," *The American Naturalist*, 770.

Vestal, Paul A., *Ethnobotany of the Ramah Navajo*, 36.

Wyman, Leland, and Stuart Harris, *Ethnobotany of the Kayenta Navajo*, 31, 61.

———, *Navajo Indian Medical Ethnobotany*, 20, 42.

Young, Stella, *Native Plants Used by the Navajo*, 8, 79, 89.

ARROWGRASS *(Triglochin)*
arrowgrass

Triglochin maritima L. (tri-'glo-chin mare-'teem-ma)
Triglochin: Three-barbed, from *tri,* "three," and *glochis,*
      "a projecting point"
maritima: Of the sea or shore

NAVAJO NAME: *Teeł łikanii,* "sweet cattail"

DESCRIPTION & DISTRIBUTION
Arrowgrass is a perennial herb with rhizomes (subterranean stems), grasslike leaves, and a leafless flowering stalk (with greenish flowers) sometimes over 1 foot tall. It resembles grasses (Poaceae sp.) and lilies (Liliaceae sp.) but is not closely related to either.

    Saline marshes below 6,000 feet are the typical habitat in which arrowgrass grows, scattered among inland saltgrass *(Distichlis stricta),* seepweeds *(Suaeda* sp.), and annual members of the saltbush genus *(Atriplex* sp.).

NAVAJO USES
MEDICINAL: Arrowgrass is used in a smoke treatment for back problems. A variety of plants are heated in a long, shallow pit. The patient lies on the vegetation and is occasionally massaged as the steam surrounds him.

    CEREMONIAL: *Teeł łikanii* is one of the grasslike plants used in the *Yé'iibicheii,* Mountaintop Way, and Shooting Way.

REFERENCES
Wyman, Leland, and Stuart Harris, *Navajo Indian Medical Ethnobotany,* 32, 36.

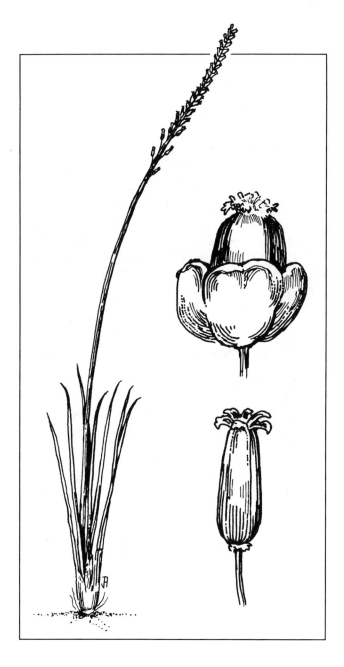

ASTER *(Leucelene)*
Manyflowered baby-aster

Leucelene ericoides (Torr.) Greene (loo-see-'lean
   air-ic-'oid-deez
Leucelene: Leuc, "white"
ericoides: From *erica,* "heather," *oides,* "like"

NAVAJO NAME: *Níí'ii'niłts' óóz,* "slender snuff"

DESCRIPTION & DISTRIBUTION
Manyflowered baby-aster is a small, perennial herb with
a woody, branching root crown. Several green stems, with
short (about ⅓ inch), linear leaves and white flowers extend a few inches upward. Flowers April through early
September.

Localized stands occur on scarified slopes up to 7,500
feet elevation. Soils are usually coarse to medium in texture.
Associates include cheatgrass *(Bromus tectorum),* six-weeks
fescue *(Vulpia octoflora),* and puccoons *(Lithospermum* sp.).

NAVAJO USES
MEDICINAL: Asters are used for snuff and to treat diseases
of the mouth. A kidney or bladder disease medicine is made
with aster and sumac *(Rhus* sp.) berries. The dried and
powdered plant is used as snuff to relieve many types of
head ailments: catarrh, swelling, sores in the nose, headache,
toothache, and sore eyes.

CEREMONIAL: *Níí'ii'nilts' óóz* is a Water Way medicine.

REFERENCES
Hocking, George M., "Some Plant Materials Used
   Medicinally and Otherwise by the Navaho Indians
   in the Chaco Canyon, New Mexico," *El Palacio,* 148.
Matthews, Washington, "Navajo Names for Plants," *The
   American Naturalist,* 773.

BARBERRY *(Berberis)*
Fremont barberry, Fremont holly-grape

Berberis fremontii Torr. ('ber-ber-iss 'free-mont-eye)
Berberis: Adaptation of an Arabic name for fruit of
      Berberis sp
fremontii: Named for one of the earliest botanists in the
      West, General John Charles Fremont,
      1813–90, an explorer, soldier, and politi-
      cian. He collected plants in the 1840s.
NAVAJO NAME: *Ché'ch'il nitł'izí yilt'ąą' ą́,* "leaves like a
      scrub oak"

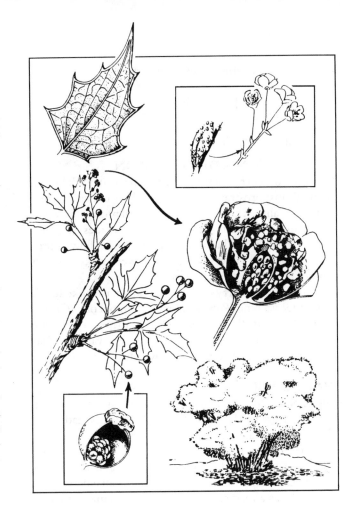

DESCRIPTION & DISTRIBUTION
Fremont barberry is an erect, rigid, evergreen shrub with
several stems rising from the ground to about 8 feet or less.
Leaves are persistent, dull green, stiff, and coarsely toothed;
teeth are sharp. Older stems have grey, shreddy bark. Small,
yellowish flowers are usually in threes. Fruits are less than
½ inch in diameter and change in color from yellow-red
to almost black. Flowers in May and June.

    Fremont barberry is found from 4,000 to 7,000 feet ele-
vation, being most common, though still infrequent, at an
elevation of 6,000 feet. Soils occupied are usually coarse to
medium texture. Vegetation type is pinyon-juniper woodland, specifically the oneseed juniper *(Juniperus monosperma)*
and Colorado pinyon *(Pinus edulis)* manifestation.

NAVAJO USES
CEREMONIAL: *Ché'ch'il nitł'izí yilt'ąą'ą́* is used in the Evil Way
and the Mountaintop Way ceremonies as an emetic.

    MEDICINAL: Fremont barberry is used for stomachache,
heartburn, and other problems connected with indigestion.
It is mixed with other plants to treat spider bites.

    OTHER: A yellow buckskin dye is made from the root
and bark of Fremont barberry.

REFERENCES
Elmore, Francis, *Ethnobotany of the Navajo,* 48.
Matthews, Washington, "Navajo Names for Plants," *The
    American Naturalist,* 770.
Wyman, Leland, and Stuart Harris, *Navajo Indian Medical
    Ethnobotany,* 21, 57, 58, 72.

creeping barberry, Oregon grape

Berberis repens Lindl. ('ber-ber-iss 'reep-ens)
repens: Creeping

NAVAJO NAME: *Tsinyaachéch'il,* "oak under a tree"

DESCRIPTION & DISTRIBUTION
Creeping barberry is a small evergreen shrub with brown stems almost prostrate so that its height is under 6 inches. Leaves are almost circular in outline with prominent veins; coarse marginal teeth are sharp; the leaf blades may turn red as early as July. Clusters of small, yellowish flowers produce purplish to violet berries that are very waxy. Flowers from April through early June.

Creeping barberry is quite common in parklike stands of ponderosa pine *(Pinus ponderosa),* Gambel oak *(Quercus gambelii),* and Rocky Mountain juniper *(Juniperus scopulorum),* between 7,000 and 8,000 feet elevation. It may extend somewhat below and above these elevations.

NAVAJO USES
MEDICINAL: Oregon grape has several Navajo medical uses. The leaves are used as a poultice, and a lotion is made from the leaves to treat scorpion bites. Leaves and twigs are used in a rheumatism medication. A tea made from the root is used as a laxative. *Berberis repens* pollen is a general cure-all.

CEREMONIAL: *Tsinyaachéch'il* is used as an emetic in the Evil Way, as a medicine in the male and female branches of the Shooting Way, and as one of several plants with berries used in the Mountaintop Way.

OTHER: For good luck, or rather, to remove bad luck, *Berberis repens* is sprinkled on grass where lightning has struck livestock. A yellow dye is made by boiling the entire plant (without berries) and using raw alum (aluminum sulfate, a mineral substance found at the base of rock cliffs on the reservation) for the mordant.

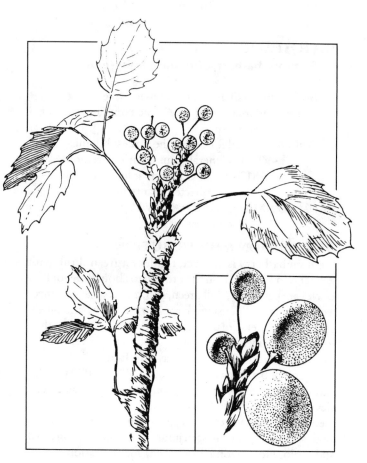

REFERENCES
Elmore, Francis, *Ethnobotany of the Navajo,* 48.
Matthews, Washington, "Navajo Names for Plants," *The American Naturalist,* 770.
Martin, Neils, *Common Range Plants,* 2.
Vestal, Paul A., *Ethnobotany of the Ramah Navajo,* 28.
Wyman, Leland, and Stuart Harris, *Ethnobotany of the Kayenta Navajo,* 23.
Young, Stella, *Native Plants Used by the Navajo,* 50, 84.

BEARD TONGUE *(Penstemon)*
bearded penstemon, scarlet penstemon

Penstemon barbatus (Cav.) Roth. (pen-'stee-mon
  bar-'bay-tuss)
Penstemon: From the Greek *pente,* "five," and *stemon,*
  "stamens"
barbatus: From the Latin *barba,* "beard"

NAVAJO NAME: *Dah yiitíhidąą,* "hummingbird food"

DESCRIPTION & DISTRIBUTION
Scarlet penstemon is an erect, perennial herb sometimes as
tall as 2½ feet. Leaves narrow as they rise on the stem. Red
snapdragon-like flowers are two-lipped (the parting "lips"
may reveal the inner stamens) and very showy. Flowers July
through early September.

Scarlet penstemon is scattered throughout its range between 6,000 and 9,000 feet but is most common at about
7,000 feet where woodland and forest overlap to form the
community of Colorado pinyon *(Pinus edulis),* Gambel oak
(Quercus gambelii), Utah juniper *(Juniperus osteosperma),* and
ponderosa pine *(Pinus ponderosa).* Embankments of medium
soil above gullies may be the best sites.

NAVAJO USES
MEDICINAL: *Dah yiitíhidąą'* is one of the life medicines (see
yarrow). It is used as a poultice on swellings, gun and arrow wounds; for stomachaches and other internal aches or
injuries; and for coughs and burns. It is an animal medication, especially for fractured or broken bones in sheep.

HOUSEHOLD: At one time, Navajos boiled scarlet
penstemon to make a sweet drink.

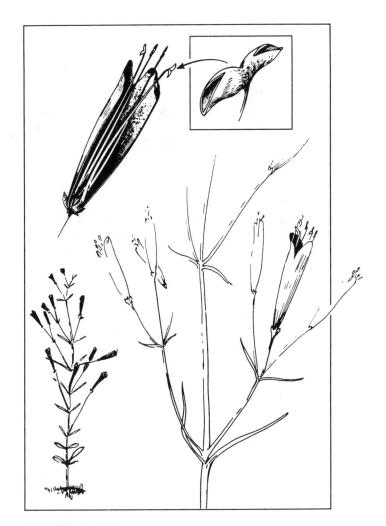

REFERENCES
Vestal, Paul A., *Ethnobotany of the Ramah Navajo,* 44.
Wyman, Leland, and Stuart Harris, *Ethnobotany of the
  Kayenta Navajo,* 42.
Young, Stella, *Native Plants Used by the Navajo,* 88.

11

BEEPLANT *(Cleome)*

Rocky Mountain beeplant, blue Colorado bee-weed, stinkflower, spider plant, guaco

Cleome serrulata Pursh (klee-'oh-mee ser-rew-'lay-tuh)
Cleome: Classical Latin name for the mustard plant
was cleome. The word's origin is Greek, *kleio,*
"to enclose," "to shut up."
serrulata: Somewhat toothed

NAVAJO NAME: *Waa',* "the beeweed"

DESCRIPTION & DISTRIBUTION

Rocky Mountain beeplant is an erect, annual herb branching a few inches above ground level when robust. Height seldom exceeds 3¼ feet. Leaves are compound and superficially resemble those of sweet clover (*Melilotus* sp.). A multitude of tiny pink to purple (rarely white) flowers are densely clustered together. Herbage is generally olive green, but stems change from yellow-green to purple-green. Flowers mid-June through early September.

Below 8,000 feet, Rocky Mountain beeplant grows along shores of washes, streams, and ponds and along roadsides and in basins; usually coarse or medium soil is occupied. In communities of ponderosa pine (*Pinus ponderosa*) and Gamble oak (*Quercus gambelii*) its associates are verbena (*Verbena* sp.), coneflower (*Ratibida* sp.), and prairie sunflower (*Helianthus petiolaris*). In communities of Colorado pinyon (*Pinus edulis*) and Utah juniper (*Juniperus osteosperma*), its associates are Texas doveweed (*Croton texensis*) and white horse-nettle (*Solanum elaeagnifolium*). In communities of black greasewood (*Sarcobatus vermiculatus*), spiny saltbush (*Atriplex confertifolia*), and rabbitbrush (*Chrysothamnus* sp.), its associates are yellow beeplant (*Cleome lutea*) and annual sunflower (*Helianthus annuus*).

NAVAJO USES

HOUSEHOLD: *Waa'* is said to have saved the Navajos from starvation and is one of the few wild foods still in use. The young plants, not more than 4 inches tall, are boiled, some say for as long as a day, then drained and boiled two more times.

The greens can be added to wild onion (*Allium* sp.), wild celery (*Apiastrum* sp.), and meat stew, fried in grease, or dried and saved for winter. The plant is also used as a food seasoning.

The seeds can be made into a mush or a bread. *See appendix, page 139, for recipe.*

An almost forgotten use of beeweed is as a firedrill. In no more time than it takes to strike a match, a fire can be started with the dry brittle twigs of beeweed. Two stalks are used. The narrower stalk, about ¼ inch thick, is turned on the edge of a small notch cut into a larger stick. A few grains of sand are placed under the drill. The friction of the drill on the sand produces a fine powder, which falls into a small pile on the ground. As the friction continues, sparks fall onto the powder. Blowing on the sparks and powder while carefully adding bark and grass starts the fire.

A yellow-green wool dye is made from fermented *waa'.* The plant is picked before it flowers and boiled until tender. Next, the cooked plant is mashed, added to a pot containing yarn, and the mixture is allowed to ferment a week. The yarn is boiled and allowed to ferment another week before being rinsed and dried.

A deodorant is made of beeweed leaves soaked in water. Beeweed leaves are placed in moccasins or shoes to remove odors.

CEREMONIAL: *Waa'* is a food and a medicine in the Night Way.

REFERENCES

Darby, William J., et al., "A Study of the Dietary Background and Nutriture of the Navajo Indians," *The Journal of Nutrition,* 21–22.

Elmore, Francis, *Ethnobotany of the Navajo,* 50–51.

Hocking, George M., "Some Plant Materials Used Medicinally and Otherwise by the Navaho Indians in the Chaco Canyon, New Mexico," *El Palacio,* 149.

Mindeleff, Cosmos, "The Navajo Reservation," *The Indian Advocate, 12,* 319–24 and *13,* 225–31.

Steggerda, Morris, and R. B. Eckardt, "Navajo Foods and Their Preparation," *American Dietetic Association Journal,* 223.

Vestal, Paul A., *Ethnobotany of the Ramah Navajo,* 29.

Wyman, Leland, and Stuart Harris, *Ethnobotany of the Kayenta Navajo,* 25, 61.

Young, Stella, *Native Plants Used by the Navajo,* 4, 26, 63–64.

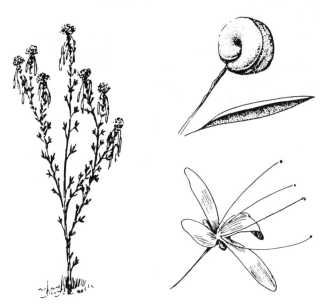

BELLFLOWER *(Campanula)*
Parry bellflower

Campanula parryi Gray (kam-'pan-yew-luh 'parry-eye)
Campanula: Sixteenth-century botanist, Leonard Fuchs,
    selected the name from the Latin word for
    bell, *campana.* It is now translated as "little
    bell."
parryi: Named for English botanist and physician Dr.
    Charles C. Parry (1823–90), who collected
    plants for the U.S.-Mexican Boundary Survey
    in 1854–58.

NAVAJO NAME: *Awéé'chí'í,* "baby newborn"

DESCRIPTION & DISTRIBUTION
Parry bellflower is an erect, single-stemmed, herbaceous
perennial growing from rhizomes (subterranean rooting
stems). Its height is usually about 6 inches but may be as
tall as 10 inches. The plant is sparsely leaved — a few leaves
at the root crown and more slender ones on the stem —
and bears one nodding, purplish blue flower at the top. It
resembles roundleaf harebell *(Campanula rotundifolia),* but
the latter is taller, has smaller but more flowers, has rounder
basal leaf blades, and more linear stem leaves. Flowers July
through early September.

Streamside and forest-park meadows at about 6,800
feet are sites for Parry bellflower. Among its frequent
associates are roundleaf harebell, western yarrow *(Achillea
millefolium),* black medic *(Medicago lupulina),* Kentucky
bluegrass *(Poa pratensis),* and bentgrasses *(Agrostis* sp.).

NAVAJO USES
CEREMONIAL: *Awéé'chí'í* is used in the Blessing Way
medicine. At one time, its blue pollen was used in many
Navajo ceremonies.

HOUSEHOLD: Parry bellflower is eaten by pregnant
Navajo women who want a daughter.

REFERENCES
Elmore, Francis, *Ethnobotany of the Navajo,* 79.
Vestal, Paul A., *Ethnobotany of the Ramah Navajo,* 47.
Wyman, Leland, and Stuart Harris, *Ethnobotany of the
    Kayenta Navajo,* 44, 61.

BINDWEED *(Convolvulus)*
field bindweed, field morning glory

Convolvulus arvensis L. (kon-volv-'yew-lus ar-'ven-siss)
Convolvulus: From the Latin *convolve,* "to roll around"
arvensis: Of cultivated fields

NAVAJO NAME: *Ch'il na'atło'ii,* "plant twining"

DESCRIPTION & DISTRIBUTION
Field bindweed, the only wild morning glory on the reservation proper, is a prostrate perennial herb with trailing, twining stems up to 2 feet long. Arrow-shaped leaves are up to 2 inches. Funnel-shaped white flowers have pink to purple marks and appear May through early September.

Field bindweed forms extensive patches on disturbed, medium soils and fine soils of depressions, roadsides, fields, and more moist sites below 8,000 feet, in association with puncture vine *(Tribulus terrestris),* prostrate pigweed *(Amaranthus graecizans),* and other weeds.

NAVAJO USES
MEDICINAL: *Ch'il na'atło'ii* is a medicine for spider bites.

REFERENCES
Elmore, Francis, *Ethnobotany of the Navajo,* 70.
Vestal, Paul A., *Ethnobotany of the Ramah Navajo,* 39.
Wyman, Leland, and Stuart Harris, *Navajo Indian Medical Ethnobotany,* 29, 44.

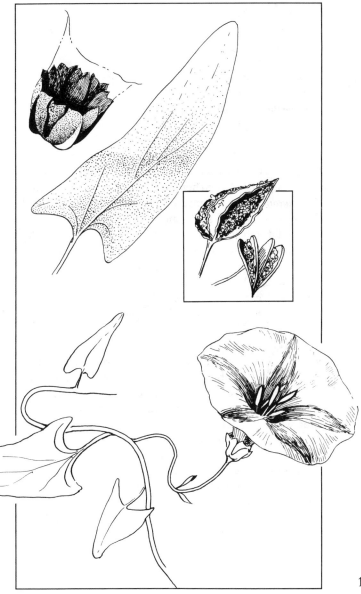

BIRCH *(Betula)*
water birch, Rocky Mountain birch, sweet birch, canyon birch

Betula occidentalis Hook ('bet-tew-luh ok-sih-den²-tay-lis)
Betula: Birch
occidentalis: Of the western hemisphere

NAVAJO NAME: *K'ishchíí,* "red alder"

DESCRIPTION & DISTRIBUTION
Water birch is a large deciduous shrub (branching from the ground) up to 20 feet in height. It resembles thinleaf alder *(Alnus incana)* but has shiny, rough, red-brown bark instead of grayish bark, and soft cones instead of woody ones.

Water birch is a constituent of riparian (streamside) vegetation between 6,000 and 9,000 feet, often on coarse soils, and in narrow canyons at the lower elevations. Close associates are thinleaf alder *(Alnus incana),* chokecherries *(Prunus* sp.), certain gooseberries *(Ribes* sp.), Rocky Mountain maple *(Acer glabrum),* and elderberries *(Sambucus* sp.).

NAVAJO USES
Water birch was used in the hoop and pole game, *na'azhǫǫzh,* or the bridging. It was played with a 6- to 9-foot, decorated birch pole and a homemade 8-inch hoop. According to the Navajo creation stories, the hoop and pole game was brought by the Navajos from the underworlds. Men played it at ceremonies, but by the early 1900s the game had almost died out.

Gambling is an essential part of Navajo games, and the determination of the stakes in *na'azhoozh* was a part of the pregame activities. *See appendix, page 139, for details of hoop and pole game.*

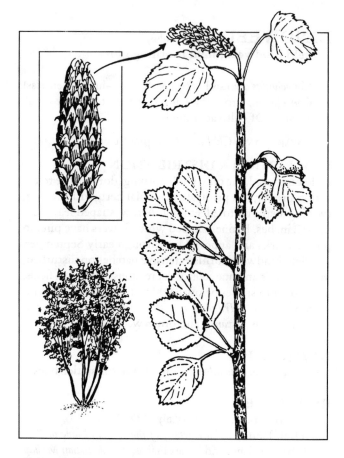

REFERENCES
Birch, Hook.

Elmore, Francis, *Ethnobotany of the Navajo,* 39–40.
Kluckhohn, Clyde, et al., *Navajo Material Culture,* 375–79.
Franciscan Fathers, *An Ethnologic Dictionary of the Navajo Language,* 482–83.

BITTERWEED *(Hymenoxys)*
Colorado rubberweed, Richardson actinea, ping-wing, pingüe

Hymenoxys richardsoni (Hook) Ckll. (hi-mee-'no-ksihs rih-kard-'so-neye)

Hymenoxys: From the Greek words *hymen,* "membrane," and *oxys,* "sharp"

richardsoni: Possibly named after Sir John Richardson (1787–1865), a Scotsman who was a naturalist, Arctic explorer, and surgeon on many western explorations.

NAVAJO NAME: *Né'éshjaa' yilkee'é,* "owllike foot"

DESCRIPTION & DISTRIBUTION
Colorado rubberweed is a perennial herb with a branched, woolly, leafy root crown. Height is about 1 foot or less. It is tufted and compact with several erect stems, most of which will bear yellow flower heads. It resembles Ives' actinea *(Hymenoxys ivesiana)* and other actineas *(Hymenoxys* sp.), but its stems are leafy and the leaves are often parted into 3 lobes. Flowers from mid-June through early September.

Colorado rubberweed is most abundant between 6,800 and 7,100 feet, where forest and woodland overlap, among Colorado pinyon *(Pinus edulis),* ponderosa pine *(Pinus ponderosa),* and big sagebrush *(Artemisia tridentata),* but its range is from about 5,000 to 8,000 feet. It grows on soils of various textures and is usually scattered rather than in dense stands.

NAVAJO USES
MEDICINAL: An internal medicine and soothing lotion for red ant bites is made from rubberweed.

CEREMONIAL: *Né'éshjaa' yilkee'é* is used as an emetic in the Evil Way ceremony.

OTHER: Colorado rubberweed root bark was used for chewing gum; the plant has a milky sap that contains latex or rubber.

Colorado rubberweed is said to be toxic to animals, especially sheep, who seem to be attracted to it.

REFERENCES
Colorado Rubberweed, (Hook.) Ckll.

Vestal, Paul A., *Ethnobotany of the Ramah Navajo,* 47.
Wyman, Leland, and Stuart Harris, *Navajo Indian Medical Ethnobotany,* 24, 31, 46.

BLACKBRUSH *(Coleogyne)*
blackbrush

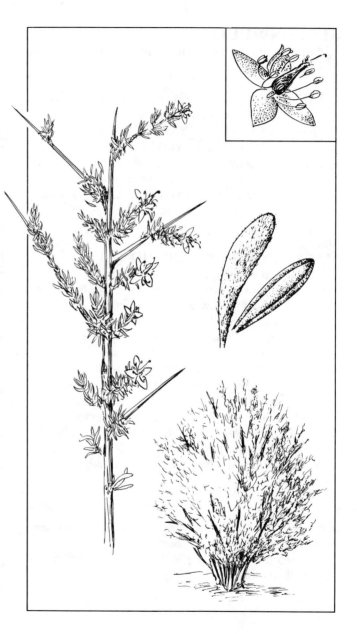

Coleogyne ramosissima Torr. (koh-lee-'ah-jih-nee
    ra-moh-'siss-sih-muh)
Coleogyne: From the Greek *koleon,* "sheath," and *gyne,*
       "female," referring to the tubular sheath that
       encloses the ovary
ramosissima: Very branched

NAVAJO NAME: *Ch'il łizhiní,* "black plant"

DESCRIPTION & DISTRIBUTION

Blackbrush is a densely branched shrub appearing quite
dark at a distance, although the leaves are dull green and
the stems are merely gray. Height seldom exceeds 3 feet.
Leaves are as long as ½ inch and seem clustered on spurs,
which eventually become thorns. Petallike parts of the
flowers are yellow above and purple below. Fruits resemble
rose hips. Flowers April through mid-May.

    The elevational range of blackbrush may be between
3,800 and 6,000 feet, but it is most abundant around 5,000
feet as the dominant of a shrubland of blackbrush, Torrey
joint-fir *(Ephedra torreyana),* goldenweed *(Aplopappus* sp.),
kochia *(Kochia* sp.), and saltbush *(Atriplex* sp.), often stabiliz-
ing sand dunes.

NAVAJO USES

Blackbrush is one of the few common plants of Navajoland
with no recorded uses.

REFERENCES

    Martin, Neils, *Common Range Plants,* 1.

BLAZING STAR *(Mentzelia)*
yellow mentzelia, stickleaf, blazing star

Mentzelia pumila (Nutt.) T. & G. (men-'zee-lee-uh
pew-'mil-uh)
Mentzelia: Named for a German botanist/physician,
Christian Mentzel (1622–1701)
pumila: Small, dwarf

NAVAJO NAME: *Íiłt'ihii,* "tenacious"

DESCRIPTION & DISTRIBUTION

Yellow mentzelia is a short-lived perennial, somewhat
woody near the base. It may grow as tall as 1½ feet.
Younger stems are green; older ones are white; the oldest
are grayish and peeling. Leaves are dull green, as long as
1½ inches, and clinging because of their roughness. Flowers are yellow and large enough to be showy. This species
closely resembles two other mentzelias that occur on the
reservation. Flowers late April through early September.

Gravelly soils of coarse or medium texture on roadsides,
embankments, and hillsides between 3,800 and 7,000 feet
are good sites for yellow mentzelia. It is distributed across
the reservation but is seldom abundant.

NAVAJO USES

MEDICINAL: Yellow mentzelia is one of the Life Medicines
(see yarrow). The flowers are made into an eyewash medication, and a lotion made from the whole plant is used to keep
smallpox sores from pitting.

CEREMONIAL: *Íiłt'ihii* is used for prayersticks in the
Beauty Way and as an Evil Way medicine.

HOUSEHOLD: The seeds can be eaten after special
preparation. First, the seed capsules are beaten to release
the seeds; then the seeds are parched with hot coals in an
old basket, and finally, ground with a special rock. The
mano, normally used for grinding seeds, is considered too
heavy to grind yellow mentzelia seeds.

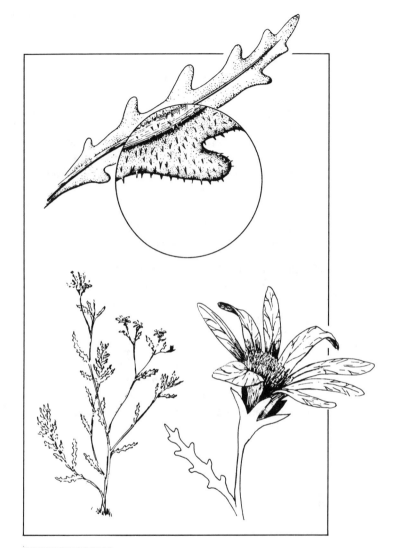

REFERENCES

Elmore, Francis, *Ethnobotany of the Navajo,* 64.
Vestal, Paul A., *Ethnobotany of the Ramah Navajo,* 37.
Wyman, Leland, and Stuart Harris, *Ethnobotany of the
Kayenta Navajo,* 32, 62.
——— , *Navajo Indian Medical Ethnobotany,* 28, 43.

19

BOX-LEAF *(Pachystima)*
mountain lover, myrtle box-leaf

Pachystima myrsinites (Pursh) Raf. (pah-'kiss-tih-muh murr-sih-'nye-teez)
Pachystima: From the Greek *pakhus,* "thick,"and *stizen,* "to prick or tattoo," now "stigma"
myrsinites: Greek for "myrtlelike." *Myrtle* sp. are aromatic shrubs native to Mediterranean and western Asiatic regions having white or pink flowers and blue-black berries.

NAVAJO NAME: *Dinasts' óóz,* "slender berry plant"

DESCRIPTION & DISTRIBUTION
Mountain lover is an evergreen shrub, sometimes simple but often very branchy and leafy, usually under 2 feet tall with semiprostrate stems bearing paired, thick leaves and inconspicuous red-brown flowers at the bases of the short leaf stalks. Flowers May through June.

Mountain forests of ponderosa pine *(Pinus ponderosa)* and Gambel oak *(Quercus gambelii)* on medium soils under some litter (plant debris) provide the sites for scattered individuals of mountain lover. It often grows in shadows without any close associates.

NAVAJO USES
CEREMONIAL: Mountain lover is used as an emetic in the Holy Way, Hand-trembling Way, Evil Way, and Male Shooting Way.

REFERENCES
Vestal, Paul A., *Ethnobotany of the Ramah Navajo,* 36.
Wyman, Leland, and Stuart Harris, *Navajo Indian Medical Ethnobotany,* 26, 42, 57–58.

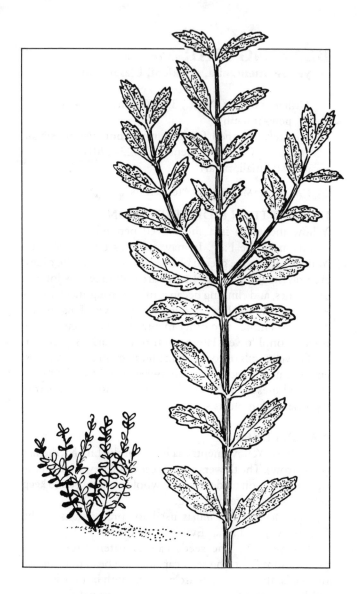

BRACKEN *(Pteridium)*
bracken fern

Pteridium aquilinum (L.) Kuhn (tehr-'rid-ee-um
    ak-wil-'lye-num)
Pteridium: Pteris, "wing," from the appearance of
    the fronds
aquilinum: From the Latin *aquila,* "edge," usually refer-
    ring to a curve or hook similar to an eagle's
    beak

NAVAJO NAME: *Dééłdą́ą́*, "crane food'

DESCRIPTION & DISTRIBUTION

Bracken fern is an herbaceous, perennial, spore-bearing
plant. From subterranean rhizomes, large fronds grow upward 2 to 3 feet above ground. Each frond is subdivided
into dull green leaflets; the midrib of each frond is yellowish. It is the only conspicuous and abundant reservation
fern.

    Edges of meadows and parks in the community of Col-
orado blue spruce *(Picea pungens),* Douglas fir *(Pseudotsuga
menziesii),* and ponderosa pine *(Pinus ponderosa)* between
7,800 and 9,000 feet are usually occupied by bracken fern.
Burns in the Colorado blue spruce and Douglas fir community are invaded by quaking aspen *(Populus tremuloides)*
and bracken fern. Other close associates are yarrow,
(Achillea millefolium), geraniums *(Geranium* sp.), and
strawberries *(Fragaria* sp.).

NAVAJO USES

MEDICINAL: Navajos use mashed bracken fern roots to treat
human or animal wounds. The fern is also an internal
medication for livestock.

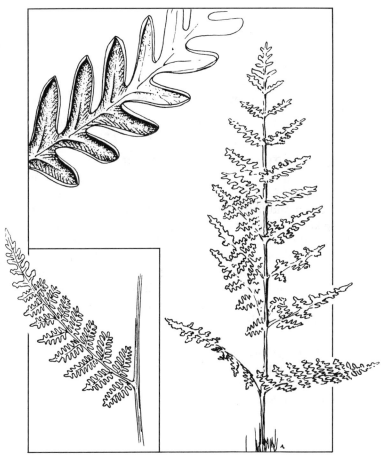

REFERENCES

Sweet, Muriel, *Common Edible and Useful Plants of the West,* 4.
Wyman, Leland, and Stuart Harris, *Navajo Indian Medical
    Ethnobotany,* 28, 35.

BROMEGRASS *(Bromus)*
cheatgrass brome, downy chess

Bromus tectorum L. ('broh-mus tek-'tohr-um)
Bromus: Greek for "oats"
tectorum: Resembling the shape of a roof

NAVAJO NAMES: *Yé'iibe'ets'os,* "God's Plume"; *Zéé'iilwo'ii,*
"mouth-enterer"

DESCRIPTION & DISTRIBUTION
Cheatgrass is an annual herb of variable size and appearance
that seldom reaches a height of 1 foot. Leaves and stems
are soft and hairy. The open cluster or arrangement of
spikelets (containing the reduced flowers) is a panicle like
that of common oats. Flowers March through July.

Adaptable weed that it is, cheatgrass invades almost all
communities on almost all soils between 4,000 and 8,000
feet elevations. Abandoned yards, fields, and dirt roads are
invariably settled by cheatgrass and Russian thistle *(Salsola
iberica),* which is equally adaptable.

NAVAJO USES
CEREMONIAL: *Yé'iibe'ets'os* is used in at least four ceremonies
other than the one for which it is named. It is used by the
God Impersonators in the Night Way chant; it is used as
a blackening in the Evil Way and Hand Trembling Way, and
as a medicine in Night Way and Plume Way.

REFERENCES
Vestal, Paul A., *Ethnobotany of the Ramah Navajo,* 16.
Wyman, Leland, and Stuart Harris, *Ethnobotany of the
Kayenta Navajo,* 15, 61.

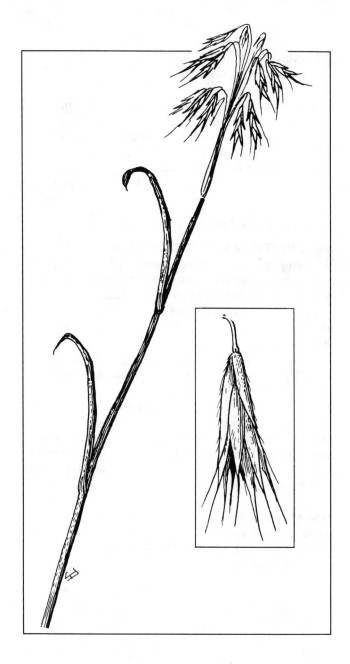

BROWN-EYED SUSAN *(Rudbeckia)*
cutleaf coneflower

Rudbeckia laciniata L. (rud-'bek-ee-uh la-sin-ee-'ay-tuh)
Rudbeckia: Named for Swedish botanist, Olans Rudbeck
      (1630–1702), who discovered the lymphatic
      system
laciniata: Cut into narrow lobes

NAVAJO NAME: *K'aasdá beeyigá nitsaaígíí,* "big-arrow-
      poison antidote"

DESCRIPTION & DISTRIBUTION
Cutleaf coneflower is a tall, leafy, erect, perennial herb,
branching above the base to bear large flower heads with
drooping yellow petallike rays and protruding rounded,
conelike, greenish yellow centers. Height may exceed 4 feet.
Lower leaves are large and are cut into several parts. Flowers
July through early September.

    Growing in medium or fine soil along streams above
6,000 feet—and probably below 8,500 feet—cutleaf coneflower associates with gooseberries *(Ribes* sp.), Arizona rose
(Rosa arizonica), goldenrods *(Solidago* sp.), and other peren-
nials of the aster (Asteraceae sp.) family.

NAVAJO USES
MEDICINAL: Cutleaf coneflower is used for heartburn, indigestion, relief from colds, and chest conjestion.
    CEREMONIAL: *K'aasdá beeyigá nitsaaígíí* is used in prayers
for rain.

REFERENCES
Wyman, Leland, and Stuart Harris, *Navajo Indian Medical
    Ethnobotany,* 29, 32, 48.

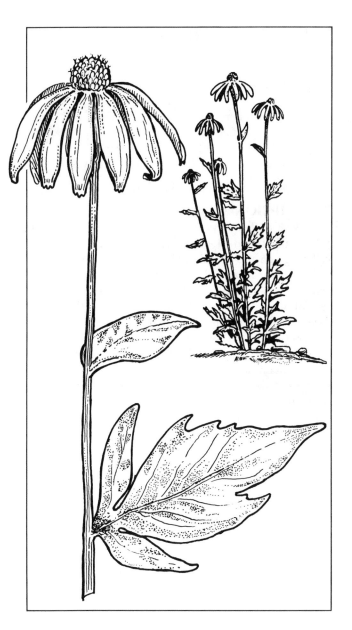

BUFFALOBERRY *(Shepherdia)*
roundleaf buffaloberry

Shepherdia rotundifolia Parry (shep-'herd-ee-uh
    roh-tun-dif-'foh-lee-uh)
Shepherdia: Named for John Shepard, (1764–1836),
        an English botanist who was curator of the
        Liverpool Botanic Gardens
rotundifolia: From the Latin for "round leaves"

NAVAJO NAME: *Dibédąą',* "sheep's food"

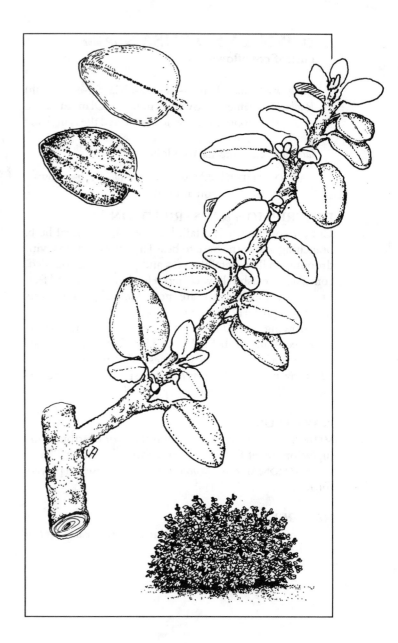

DESCRIPTION & DISTRIBUTION
Roundleaf buffaloberry is a dense, compact shrub about
3 feet tall. The thick leaves are gray-green above and
yellow-green and densely fuzzy below; length is up to 1
inch. Stems are fuzzy white when young, becoming fuzzy
pale yellow and finally dark as they age. Superficially, it
resembles its relative the Russian olive *(Elaeagnus
angustifolia)* only in foliage and in flower color. Pale yellow
flowers bloom in May and June.

    Although it is locally abundant on south slopes of some
tall mountains at about 9,300 feet and ranges down into
canyons at about 4,000 feet, it is not widely distributed
across the reservation. Common associates may be other
shrubs such as curlleaf mountain mahogany *(Cercocarpus
ledifolius),* and Utah snowberry *(Symphoricarpos utahensis).*

NAVAJO USES
MEDICINAL: The ashes of roundleaf buffaloberry are made
into a lotion to soothe headaches, toothaches, sorethroats,
and to heal a baby's navel.
    CEREMONIAL: *Dibédąą'* is a Plume Way emetic.

REFERENCES
Martin, Neils, *Common Range Plants,* 3.
Wyman, Leland, and Stuart Harris, *Ethnobotany of the
    Kayenta Navajo,* 32.

CATTAIL *(Typha)*
southern cattail

Typha domingensis Pers. ('tye-fuh do-min-'gen-siss)
Typha: Greek for "cattail," also used to mean plant used
    to stuff beds, such as the cattail
domingensis: Of or from Santo Domingo

NAVAJO NAME: *Teeł nitsaaígíí,* "big cattail"

DESCRIPTION & DISTRIBUTION
Southern cattail, a very tall, perennial herb, grows well above shallow water from rhizomes in the mud; dark green, narrow, linear leaves and the stalks bearing long, slender spikes (cattails) may reach upward almost 6 feet above the root crown. It resembles broadleaved cattail *(Typha latifolia)* but is shorter and has narrower leaves and a gap in the spike or cattail (which is also relatively lighter in color).

In shallow water of sewage lagoons, ponds, and drainage ditches of the eastern sector of the reservation below about 5,500 feet, southern cattail associates with bulrushes *(Scirpus* sp.), burreeds *(Sparganium* sp.), and broadleaved cattail.

NAVAJO USES
CEREMONIAL: At one time, *teeł nitsaaígíí* pollen was preferred in Navajo ceremonies. Today corn pollen is used. *Teeł nitsaaígíí* leaves are used for ceremonial necklaces and wristbands in the Male Shooting Way. It is one of the emetics used in the five- and nine-night ceremonies.

HOUSEHOLD: It is said that male and female mats made of cattail leaves were hung in hogans to keep the hogan and livestock safe from lightning.

Unlike other Indian peoples, Navajos never ate this edible plant.

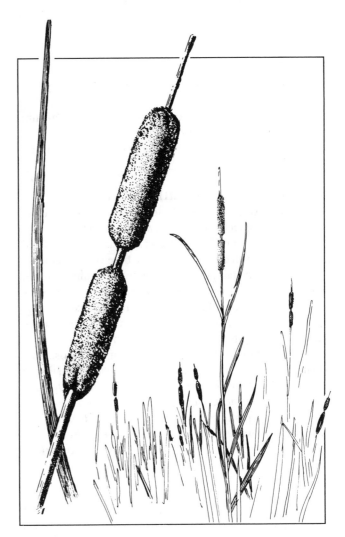

REFERENCES
Elmore, Francis, *Ethnobotany of the Navajo,* 24.
Wyman, Leland, and Stuart Harris, *Navajo Indian Medical Ethnobotany,* 32, 36, 57–58.

CHERRY *(Prunus)*
common chokecherry, western chokecherry

Prunus virginiana L. ('prew-nuss verr-gih-nih-'a-nuh)
Prunus: From the Latin word for plum, *pruna*
virginiana: Of or from the original Virginia territory

NAVAJO NAME: *Shashdąą',* "bear's food"

DESCRIPTION & DISTRIBUTION

Common chokecherry is a deciduous shrub or small tree seldom over 10 feet tall. Young twigs are brown; old bark on the trunk is gray. Leaves are as long as 2½ inches and have finely toothed margins. At the base of the blade on the petiole (leaf stalk) there are two tiny, purplish bumps. The white flowers are clustered on green stems and produce purplish fruits. Flowers April through early June.

In Navajoland, common chokecherry seems to be sparsely distributed along streams or on northern mountain slopes above 7,000 feet in forests of ponderosa pine *(Pinus ponderosa)*, Gambel oak *(Quercus gambelii)*, and Rocky Mountain juniper *(Juniperus scopulorum)*; and of Douglas fir *(Pseudotsuga menziesii)*, Colorado blue spruce *(Picea pungens)*, and quaking aspen *(Populus tremuloides)*. Its close associates, however, are snowberries *(Symphoricarpos* sp.), Rocky Mountain maple *(Acer glabrum)*, Arizona rose *(Rosa arizonica)*, and gooseberries *(Ribes* sp.).

NAVAJO USES

CEREMONIAL: *Shashdąą'* is sacred to the Navajos. Its wood is used to make many ceremonial items, such as hoops and prayersticks. A stylized chokecherry branch is represented in one of the sandpaintings of the Mountain Chant. It is also used for ceremonial medicine and as a ceremonial emetic.

HOUSEHOLD: The purplish fruit can be eaten raw or cooked with cornmeal. The roots are used to make a brown dye.

26

REFERENCES

Elmore, Francis, *Ethnobotany of the Navajo,* 54.
Martin, Neils, *Common Range Plants,* 1.
Wyman, Leland, and Stuart Harris, *Navajo Indian Medical Ethnobotany,* 25, 30, 41, 57–58, 72–73.
Young, Stella, *Native Plants Used by the Navajo,* 13, 58.

CLIFFROSE *(Cowania)*
common cliffrose, quinine bush

Cowania mexicana D. Don (kow-'way-nih-uh
    mex-ik-'kay-nuh)
Cowania: Named for James Cowan (d. 1823), a British
            merchant and amateur botanist who intro-
            duced many plants from Mexico and Peru
            into England
mexicana: Of or from Mexico

NAVAJO NAME: *Awééts'áál,* "baby cradle"

DESCRIPTION & DISTRIBUTION
Common cliffrose is not a wild rose but merely a relative
in the same family. It is similar in appearance to Apache
plume *(Fallugia paradoxa)* and bitterbush *(Purshia* sp.). Cliffrose is a straggly, evergreen shrub usually under 7 feet high.
Bark is shreddy and very soft. As the white flowers wither,
about 5 feathery plumes develop from their centers.
Flowers late April through late August.

Isolated stands of common cliffrose are scattered in the
shrublands and woodlands between about 4,500 feet and
6,800 feet on steep slopes, hillsides, cliffsides, and canyon
rims. Close associates are Utah serviceberry *(Amelanchier
utahensis),* alderleaf mountain mahogany *(Cercocarpus montanus),* and cliff fendlerbush *(Fendlera rupicola).*

NAVAJO USES
MEDICINAL: Quinine bush is an emetic and is used for
stomachache and nausea. It is also made into a lotion for
skin problems and bites of venomous animals. The leaves
are made into a cough syrup.

CEREMONIAL: *Awééts'áál* is used as a food in the Navajo
Wind Way, Night Chant, Shooting Way, and Plume Way,
and as an emetic in many ceremonies. Singers use it as an
emetic in the sweathouse to improve their voices. It is
substituted for cliff fendlerbush, if the patient is female, in

27

many ceremonies. Ceremonial prayersticks and arrows are made from *awééts'áál.*

OTHER: The evergreen twigs may be picked for dye at any time of year. *See appendix, page 140, for gold dye recipe.*

Pounded branches and twigs of *awééts'áál* and juniper (*Juniperus* sp.) make a yellow, brown, or tan dye.

Cliffrose's young, shreddy bark was once used to line the cradleboard. The shredded bark was more absorbent than cotton and could be reused after drying in the sun.

Cowania mexicana provides forage for deer and livestock.

REFERENCES
Dodge, Natt, *100 Desert Wildflowers in Natural Color,* 23.

Elmore, Francis, *Ethnobotany of the Navajo,* 53.

Franciscan Fathers, *An Ethnologic Dictionary of the Navajo Language,* 197, 470–71, 484–85.

Hocking, George M., "Some Plant Materials Used Medicinally and Otherwise by the Navaho Indians in the Chaco Canyon, New Mexico," *El Palacio,* 159–60.

Martin, Neils, *Common Range Plants,* 2.

Matthews, Washington, "Navajo Names for Plants," *The American Naturalist,* 772.

Vestal, Paul A., *Ethnobotany of the Ramah Navajo,* 30.

Wyman, Leland, and Stuart Harris, *Ethnobotany of the Kayenta Navajo,* 26, 61.

———, *Navajo Indian Medical Ethnobotany,* 18, 41, 57–58.

Young, Stella, and N. G. Bryan, *Navajo Native Dyes,* 60.

Young, Stella, *Native Plants Used by the Navajo,* 47, 72, 104.

COCKLEBUR (*Xanthium*)
common cocklebur, sheepbur, buttonbur, clothbur, ditchbur

Xanthium strumarium L. ('zan-thy-yum stru-'may-rye-um)
Xanthium: From *xanthos,* a word meaning "shades of yellow"
strumarium: From a botanical word *struma,* the cushion-like swellings at the base of a moss capsule

NAVAJO NAME: *Ta'neets'éhii,* "burs"

DESCRIPTION & DISTRIBUTION
Common cocklebur is a bristly, annual herb 1 to 3 feet tall with maroon-blotched stems, sunflowerlike leaves, and prickly heads. Small seedlings resemble those of annual sunflowers (*Helianthus* sp.). The heads of burs readily cling to passersby. Flowers June through October.

Sporadically flooded sites, with coarse to medium soils, up to about 6,800 feet elevation may be occupied by common cocklebur and its associates: pigweeds (*Amaranthus* sp.), sunflowers (*Helianthus* sp.), kochia (*Kochia* sp.), smotherweed (*Bassia* sp.), Rocky Mountain beeplant (*Cleome serrulata*), and Texas doveweed (*Croton texensis*).

NAVAJO USES
A liniment made of the cocklebur is rubbed under the armpit to remove excessive perspiration.

REFERENCES
Elmore, Francis, *Ethnobotany of the Navajo,* 90.

Matthews, Washington, "Navajo Names for Plants," *The American Naturalist,* 773.

Young, Stella, *Native Plants Used by the Navajo,* 86.

COTTONWOOD *(Populus)*
Fremont cottonwood, Fremont poplar

Populus fremontii S. Wats. ('pop-yew-lus 'free-mont-eye)
Populus: Named by one of the Pliny's [there was an Elder (A.D. 23–79) and a Younger (A.D. 61–105)]. The Turin Poplar was frequently planted in Roman cities, thus giving it the name *arbor-populi,* "tree of the people."
fremontii: Named for one of the earliest botanists in the West, General John Charles Fremont, (1813–90). He was Governor of the Arizona Territory from 1878–82 and one of the first senators from California. He collected plants in the 1840s.

NAVAJO NAME: *T'iis bit'ąą' niteelígíí,* "broadleaf cottonwood"

DESCRIPTION & DISTRIBUTION
Fremont cottonwood, one of the poplars, is a deciduous tree as tall as 60 feet with a stout trunk as broad as 3½ feet; twigs are tan, but the bark becomes grayish as it ages. Decadence seems to occur at 70 to 75 years and then large boughs break during and after winds. The small fruits clustered on female trees split and release hairy seeds May through June.

Riparian communities along washes, streams, and lakes are usually dominated by Fremont cottonwood below 6,800 feet. Conspicuous among its woody associates are Russian olive *(Eleagnus angustifolia),* tamarisk *(Tamarix chinensis),* western black willow *(Salix gooddingii),* coyote willow *(Salix exigua),* and red willow *(Salix laevigata).*

NAVAJO USES

CEREMONIAL: Small ceremonial figurines are carved from cottonwood roots.

OTHER: Cottonwood was the source of many household and game items. Some of the earliest saddles had leather covered cottonwood or pinyon bases. Cottonwood was made into cradleboards, snowshoes, shovels and hoes, and was used to build the sweathouse. Lances were made of cottonwood.

A flat piece of cottonwood, about a foot long, was used for a fire hearth. Dry juniper *(Juniperus* sp.) bark was piled around the hearth, as the cottonwood or sagebrush *(Artemisia* sp.) drill was twirled in one of its several small pits. The resulting sparks would land in the juniper kindling and start the fire. Cottonwood makes a good summer fire because it gives light without heat.

Dice in at least two Navajo games are made of cottonwood. *See appendix, page 140, for games' details.*

REFERENCES

Elmore, Francis, *Ethnobotany of the Navajo,* 38.

Franciscan Fathers, *An Ethnologic Dictionary of the Navajo Language,* 47, 66, 148, 198, 272, 415, 495–97.

Kluckhohn, Clyde, et al., *Navajo Material Culture,* 84, 136, 166, 172, 195, 320, 333, 401, 416.

Matthews, Washington, "Navajo Names for Plants," *The American Naturalist,* 776.

Wyman, Leland, and Stuart Harris, *Navajo Indian Medical Ethnobotany,* 32.

Young, Stella, *Native Plants Used by the Navajo,* 33.

CROTON *(Croton)*
Texas doveweed, Texas croton

Croton texensis (Klotzsch) Muell. ('kro-ton tex-'en-siss)
Croton: Greek name for "tick." The seeds of some of the
    species are said to look like an engorged tick.
texensis: Of or from Texas

NAVAJO NAME: *Na'ashjé'iidą̄ą̄,* "spider food"

DESCRIPTION & DISTRIBUTION
Texas doveweed is a malodorous, annual herb attaining
heights up to about 3 feet. Herbage is covered with asterisk-
like hairs. Some specimens superficially resemble slimleaf
goosefoot *(Chenopodium leptophyllum).* White flowers bloom
June through August.

Ranging up to elevations of about 7,000 feet, Texas
doveweed is most common between 5,500 and 6,500 feet
in association with Rocky Mountain beeplant *(Cleome serrulata).* It is found on coarse to medium soils along roadsides and washes, and in swales or basins within the Colorado pinyon *(Pinus edulis)* and Utah juniper *(Juniperus
osteosperma)* community, and in the Fremont cottonwood
(Populus fremontii) and common Russian olive *(Elaeagnus
angustifolia)* community.

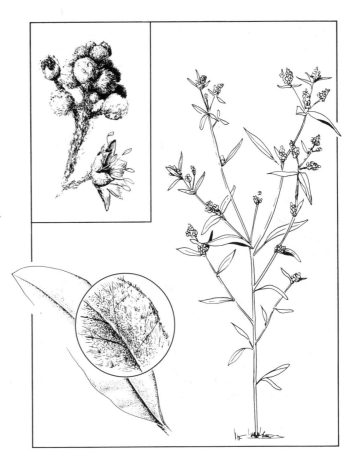

NAVAJO USES
MEDICINAL: Texas doveweed is used as a remedy for the
bites of venomous spiders and insects, such as black widow
spiders and black beetles. It is made into a lotion and drunk
or rubbed on the sore. Sand verbena *(Abronia* sp.) is added
to the medicine for black beetle bites.

CEREMONIAL: *Na'ashjé'iidą̄ą̄* is a medicine and a body
paint in the Shooting Way.

OTHER: The strong odor of Texas doveweed is used to
remove a skunk smell from clothes. The plant is added to
a large fire and clothes are held in the smoke.

REFERENCES
Elmore, Francis, *Ethnobotany of the Navajo,* 60.
Franciscan Fathers, *An Ethnologic Dictionary of the Navajo
    Language,* 189.
Vestal, Paul A., *Ethnobotany of the Ramah Navajo,* 35.
Wyman, Leland, and Stuart Harris, *Ethnobotany of the
    Kayenta Navajo,* 30, 61.
——— , *Navajo Indian Medical Ethnobotany,* 30, 42, 65–66.

CROWNBEARD *(Verbesina)*
golden crownbeard, goldenbeard, goldweed

Verbesina encelioides (Cav.) Benth. and Hook. (ver-bes-
'sye-nuh in-see-lee-'oy-dees)
Verbesina: Named for its resemblance to verbena, a
sacred herb of the Romans
encelioides: Named after a South American member of
the Asteraceae family, *Encelia* sp., *oides*,
means "having the shape of"

NAVAJO NAME: *nidíyílii łibáhígíí, "gray sunflower"*

DESCRIPTION & DISTRIBUTION
Golden crownbeard is an erect annual herb up to about 3
feet tall. Often there is one main stem from the root crown;
it may branch toward its apex. Stems are somewhat grayish
and hairy; leaves are yellow-green and rough above,
covered with pressed, whitish hairs below. Yellow-orange
flowers bloom July through September.

Although ranging between 4,000 feet and 7,750 feet elevations, it is most common at about 6,500 feet in shrublands,
basins, or swales on soils of coarse to medium textures.
Communities of black greasewood *(Sarcobatus vermiculatus)*
and shadscale *(Atriplex confertifolia)* and fourwing saltbush
(Atriplex canescens) and rabbitbrushes *(Chrysothamnus* sp.),
and big sagebrush *(Artemisia tridentata)* and snakeweeds
(Gutierrezia sp.) are its preferred neighborhoods.

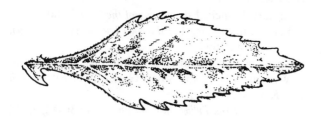

NAVAJO USES

MEDICINAL: The crushed dried leaves of *Verbesina encelioides* are mixed with water and the strained liquid used for stomach troubles. The same mixture is used internally and externally as a medicine for spider bites.

CEREMONIAL: *Verbesina encelioides* is used for medicine in the Beauty Way, and for prayersticks in Night Way and Plume Way.

OTHER: According to legend, when someone tried to kill the horned lizard, he ran under a *nidíyílii łibáhígíí*. Although lightning struck on all sides, neither the horned lizard nor the plant were hit.

Today, golden crownbeard is a good luck token. Hung upside down in the hogan it is said to stave off lightning. Hunters chew the petals for good hunting.

An old remedy for cutworms in corn was to put four worms in a dried golden crownbeard stem and set it on the edge of a Pueblo ruin. When the worms had disappeared, the stem was buried, the spot covered with a pottery sherd and a line drawn around it with an arrowhead.

The Navajos are said to have eaten the seeds of *Verbesina encelioides*.

REFERENCES

Elmore, Francis, *Ethnobotany of the Navajo*, 90.

Matthews, Washington, "Navajo Names for Plants," *The American Naturalist*, 767.

Vestal, Paul A., *Ethnobotany of the Ramah Navajo*, 54.

Wyman, Leland, and Stuart Harris, *Ethnobotany of the Kayenta Navajo*, 51, 61.

———— , *Navajo Indian Medical Ethnobotany*, 31, 48, 72.

Young, Stella, *Native Plants Used by the Navajo*, 80, 98.

DOCK *(Rumex)*
curly-leaf dock, sorrel

Rumex crispus L. ('roo-mex 'krisp-us)
Rumex: Classical name given this genus
crispus: Curled or undulating

NAVAJO NAME: *Ch'il bikétł' óól łitsooígíí*, "plant with yellow root"

DESCRIPTION & DISTRIBUTION

Curly-leaf dock is an herbaceous perennial with a single stem. Large leaves clustered at the base and smaller ones farther up the stem superficially resemble those of Swiss chard *(Beta vulgaris* var. *cicla)* in shape and have very ruffled margins. The plant is dull green and is usually under 3 feet tall. Flowers are tiny and inconspicuous; they produce winged fruits that become rosy in color. Similar and related species are canaigre *(Rumex hymenosepalus)*, and Mexican dock *(Rumex mexicanus)*. Flowers from late March through early October.

Curly-leaf dock grows along streams, irrigation ditches, pond shores, and margins of frequently irrigated fields, below about 8,500 feet. Associates are plantains *(Plantago* sp.), other docks *(Rumex* sp.), knotweeds *(Polygonum* sp.), horsetails *(Equisetum* sp.), sedges *(Carex* sp.), and rushes *(Juncus* sp.).

NAVAJO USES

MEDICINAL: The root of curly-leaf dock is one of the Navajo life medicines (see yarrow). The root and dried leaves are used on sores; a liquid made of the dried leaves mixed with water is used for sores in the mouth. The plant is used to revive someone who has fainted.

CEREMONIAL: *Ch'il bikétł' óól łitsooígíí* is a Holy Way and Lightning Way emetic.

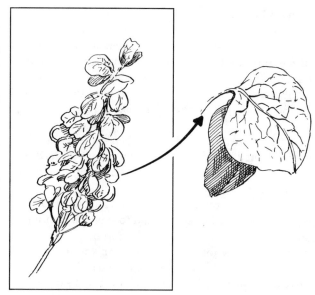

REFERENCES

Hocking, George M., "Some Plant Materials Used Medicinally and Otherwise by the Navaho Indians in the Chaco Canyon, New Mexico," *El Palacio,* 155, 157, 163.

Vestal, Paul A., *Ethnobotany of the Ramah Navajo,* 24.

Wyman, Leland, and Stuart Harris, *Navajo Indian Medical Ethnobotany,* 24–25, 38, 68.

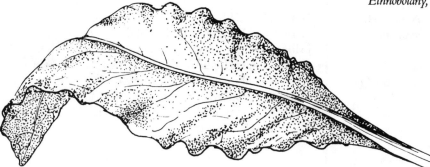

DOGWOOD *(Cornus)*
creeping dogwood, redosier dogwood

Cornus stolonifera Michx. ('kor-nuss stoh-luh-'nih-feh-ruh)
Cornus: From the Latin word for horn, *cornus,* referring to the tough hard wood of the European Cornelian cherry *(Cornus mas),* which was used for spears, shafts, and javelins.
stolonifera: To form stolons (a stem growing underground and taking root at nodes or apex to form new plants)

NAVAJO NAME: *K'ai' łichí'ii,* "red willow"

DESCRIPTION & DISTRIBUTION
Creeping dogwood is a semierect to sprawling shrub with drooping red-brown stems usually under 6 feet tall. Leaves are deciduous and as long as 3 inches. Tiny white flowers are in dense clusters. Fruits are pale, almost whitish. Creeping dogwood resembles silktassle bush *(Garrya* sp.), which may also occur on the reservation but in different habitats. Flowers May through early July.

Narrow canyons, below 7,000 feet, and mountain passes, up to 8,500 feet, with streams are the common places inhabited by redosier dogwood, in association with willows *(Salix* sp.), water birch *(Betula occidentalis),* thinleaf alder *(Alnus incana),* and other shrubs.

NAVAJO USES
CEREMONIAL: *K'ai' łichí'ii* is used as an Evil Way emetic and for Evil Way hoops, as a Mountaintop Way emetic and medicine, and for Big Star Way hoops.

REFERENCES
Vestal, Paul A., *Ethnobotany of the Ramah Navajo,* 38.
Wyman, Leland, and Stuart Harris, *Ethnobotany of the Kayenta Navajo,* 35, 62.

EVENING PRIMROSE *(Oenothera)*
white-stemmed evening primrose

Oenothera albicaulis Pursh. (ee-noh-'theer-uh
    al-bih-'kaw-liss)
Oenothera: From the Greek *oinos,* "wine," and *thera,*
        "drinking alcohol" (the roots of *Oenothera* sp.
        were thought to lead people to drink)
albicaulis: White-stemmed; *albi,* the Latin word for
        "white," and *caulis,* the Greek word for "stem"

NAVAJO NAME: *Tł'éé' íigahiits'óóz,* "white at night"

DESCRIPTION & DISTRIBUTION
White-stemmed evening primrose is a semierect, annual
herb as tall as 1½ feet but more often about 1 foot. Whitish
stems bear dull green leaves and showy white flowers (turning pinkish or purplish as they wither), open from midaf-
ternoon until midmorning. They resemble several other
long-stemmed, white-flowered evening primroses
(Oenothera sp.). Flowers late April through early September.

    Below about 7,750 feet, white-stemmed evening prim-
rose grows in small colonies scattered along roadsides, wash
embankments, and around dunes. The primroses grow
with white-flowered wild mustards (Cruciferae sp.).

NAVAJO USES
MEDICINAL: White-stemmed evening primrose is used as
a lotion for boils. It is mixed with flax *(Linum aristatum)* and
nodding eriogonum *(Eriogonum cernuum)* to treat kidney
disease. The whole plant is used as a poultice on spider bites,
and the ground plant is used as a dusting powder on sores.

    CEREMONIAL: *Tł'éé' íigahiits'óóz* is used as a Bead Way
emetic and Big Star Way, Red Ant Way, and Blessing Way
medicines.

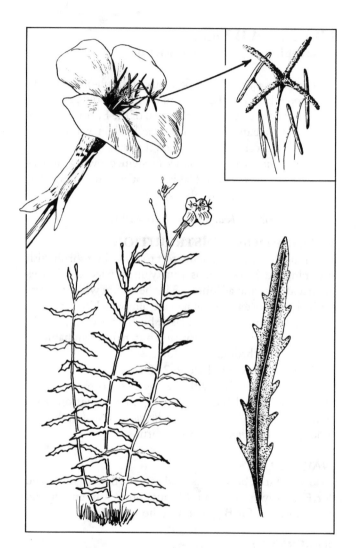

REFERENCES
Vestal, Paul A., *Ethnobotany of the Ramah Navajo,* 37.
Wyman, Leland, and Stuart Harris, *Navajo Indian Medical
    Ethnobotany,* 18, 33, 43.

FIR *(Abies)*
subalpine fir

Abies lasiocarpa (Hook.) Arn. ('ay-beez lay-see-oh-'karp-uh)
Abies: Silver fir tree
lasiocarpa: Rough or hairy fruited

NAVAJO NAME: *Ch'ółgaii,* "white Douglas fir"

DESCRIPTION & DISTRIBUTION

Subalpine fir is a symmetrical, spirelike, evergreen conifer reaching heights of about 60 feet. Branches extend down to the ground around boles (trunks) of young trees. Twigs are gray and become blistered as they age; older bark is gray, but tinged tan, and scaly. The rather flexible, flattened, blunt needles are blue-gray-green, curved, and single. Cones are upright, deep violet-blue (almost black), and about 3 inches long.

From the highest elevations of Navajoland—about 10,400—atop the tallest peaks, subalpine fir ranges downward to about 9,000 feet. With limber pine *(Pinus flexilis)* and Engelmann spruce *(Picea engelmannii),* it forms the community dominating the mountaintops. Its other associates are quaking aspen *(Populus tremuloides)* and Douglas fir *(Pseudotsuga menziesii)* on the slopes.

NAVAJO USES

CEREMONIAL: Evergreen branches are part of the dancers' dress in the *Yé'iibicheii* (Night Way) and fire dances (Mountain Way).

OTHER: In Navajo culture, fir is associated with bad winds like tornados. Because of this, it is not used for household items or construction unless proper offerings are made. When this is done, the tall straight trees are ideal for tepee poles or looms.

REFERENCES

Personal communication, June 1979.

37

FOUR O'CLOCK *(Mirabilis)*
Colorado four o'clock, manyflowered four o'clock

Mirabilis multiflora (Torr.) Gray. (mihr-'rab-il-iss
  mult-if-'floh-ruh)
Mirabilis: From the Latin *mirabilis,* "marvelous" and
  "strange"
multiflora: Manyflowered

NAVAJO NAME: *Tsédédééh,* "falling-on-rock"

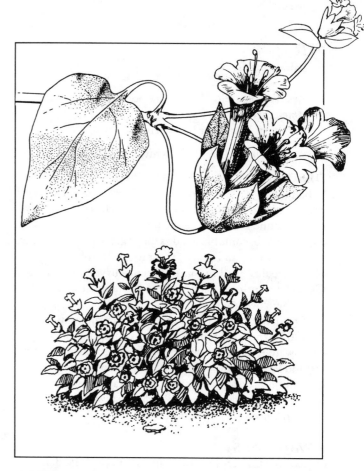

DESCRIPTION & DISTRIBUTION
Colorado four o'clock is an herbaceous perennial with stout
semiprostrate to semierect stems up to 1 foot in height and
about 2½ feet in length. Stems and leaves are gray-green
and waxy. Leaves may be up to 2½ inches long and almost
that broad. Flowers are blue-red or magenta and about 2
inches long. Flowers mostly from June through August.

Below 6,500 feet elevation, Colorado four o'clock is
scattered on firm embankments, at bases of boulders, and
along roadsides in woodlands, shrublands, and bare, eroded
areas like Nazlini and Monument Valley.

NAVAJO USES
MEDICINAL: Colorado four o'clock is used for sores in the
mouth (canker sore, swollen gums, or decayed teeth) and
for rheumatism and swellings. It is also used to treat broken
bones in humans and animals.

OTHER: A light red dye can be made from the petals of
this four o'clock if the petals are boiled no more than fifteen
minutes. It is an uncertain dye: if it boils longer, it becomes
a muddy yellowish color, and the wool may turn a peculiar
shade of light brown or even purple.

Ramah Navajos make a tea from *tsédédééh.*

REFERENCES
Elmore, Francis, *Ethnobotany of the Navajo,* 46.
Franciscan Fathers, *An Ethnologic Dictionary of the Navajo
  Language,* 195.
Hocking, George M., "Some Plant Materials Used
  Medicinally and Otherwise by the Navaho Indians
  in the Chaco Canyon, New Mexico," *El Palacio,* 161.
Vestal, Paul A., *Ethnobotany of the Ramah Navajo,* 26.
Wyman, Leland, and Stuart Harris, *Navajo Indian Medical
  Ethnobotany,* 21, 33, 39, 55, 58–59.

GALLETA *(Hilaria)*
galleta

Hilaria jamesii (Torr.) Benth. (hi-'lay-ree-uh 'jaymz-eye)
Hilaria: Named for St. Hilaire, a botanist and author
    (A.D. 315–67)
jamesii: Named for Dr. Edwin James (1797–1861), a
    physician-botanist-historian who explored the
    West in the 1800s

NAVAJO NAME: *Tł'oh łichí'í*, "red grass"

DESCRIPTION & DISTRIBUTION

Galleta is a tough, perennial grass with rhizomes from which shoots grow in patches. Height is less than 2 feet. The gray-green leaves are somewhat stiff, narrow, and rolled along the edges. Old leaf sheaths at the base of the plant are yellowish. The young florets of the spike soon become pale purple. Flowers from late April through August.

Galleta is the second most abundant perennial grass in Navajoland. Its elevational range is from the lowest points of the reservation up to about 6,800 feet. A major constituent in the shrubland of spiny saltbush *(Atriplex confertifolia)* and Torrey joint-fir *(Ephedra torreyana)*, in the shrubland of big sagebrush *(Artemisia tridentata)* and fourwing saltbush *(Atriplex canescens)*, and in the woodland of Colorado pinyon *(Pinus edulis)* and junipers *(Juniperus sp.)*, it occupies more ground than does blue grama *(Bouteloua gracilis)* at lower elevations but yields to the latter at about 5,500 feet. Most frequent associates are blue grama, western wheatgrass *(Agropyron smithii)*, and sand dropseed *(Sporobolus cryptandrus)*.

NAVAJO USES

HOUSEHOLD: Mothers give a tea of *tł'oh łichí'í* to babies so they will be strong adults.

REFERENCES

Elmore, Francis, *Ethnobotany of the Navajo*, 25.
Vestal, Paul A., *Ethnobotany of the Ramah Navajo*, 16.
Young, Stella, *Native Plants Used by the Navajo*, 70.

GILIA *(Gilia)*
few-leaved gilia

Gilia subnuda Torr. ('hill-ee-uh sub-'new-duh)
Gilia: Named for Phillip Gillio, a Spanish botanist
subnuda: Sub, "almost" and *nudus,* "naked"

NAVAJO NAME: *Hózhǫ́ǫ́jí nát'oh bit'ąą' łichí'ígíí,* "red leaf
Blessing Way tobacco"

DESCRIPTION & DISTRIBUTION

Few-leaved gilia is an herb and probably biennial. Usually a single stem arises from the root crown a few inches, branches, and attains a height of about 1 foot or less. Stems are green at the top of the plant and purple-blotched at the base. Leaves clustered at the base soon turn purple; they may be as long as 1½ inches and toothed. Foliage is somewhat sticky. Flowers are red-purple to red-pink and may be as long as ⅞ of an inch. Flowers May through June.

Medium-textured soils on slopes, embankments, cliffs, and hillsides at elevations of about 6,500 feet seem to be the best sites for few-leaved gilia, especially when the ground is almost bare, but the species ranges up to 7,500 and down to 5,000 feet. The plants are scattered over the site; associates are few.

NAVAJO USES

MEDICINAL: Pregnant women eat the ground-up flowers to insure they will have a healthy pregnancy and an easy delivery. Few-leaved gilia is also used for indigestion.

CEREMONIAL: *Hózhǫ́ǫ́jí nát'oh bit'ąą' łichí'ígíí* is a Blessing Way medicine.

REFERENCES

Hocking, George M., "Some Plant Materials Used Medicinally and Otherwise by the Navaho Indians in the Chaco Canyon, New Mexico," *El Palacio,* 160–61.

Wyman, Leland, and Stuart Harris, *Ethnobotany of the Kayenta Navajo,* 38.

——— , *Navajo Indian Medical Ethnobotany,* 56, 62.

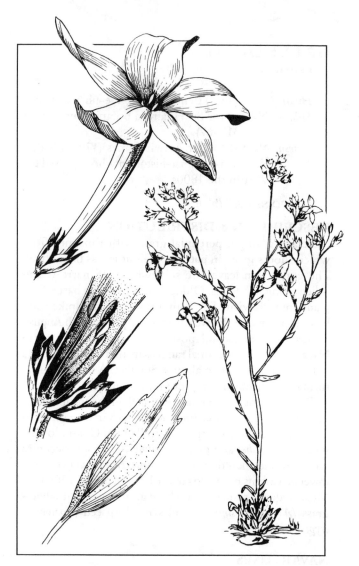

GOATSBEARD *(Tragopogon)*
oyster plant, salsify

Tragopogon dubius Scop. (trag-oh-'poh-gon 'dew-bee-us)
Tragopogon: From the Greek, *tragos,* "he-goat" (which
came from *trago,* "to nibble"); and *pogon,*
"beard," referring to the long silky beards
of the seed
dubius: From the Latin *dubious,* "uncertain"

NAVAJO NAME: *Ch'il abe'é,* "milky plant"

DESCRIPTION & DISTRIBUTION

Goatsbeard is a perennial herb with erect stems about 2 feet
tall and 6-inch or shorter grasslike leaves. Herbage is dull
green and partly covered with a loose, whitish, cobwebby
mat. Rays (peripheral petallike flowers) of the head are
yellow and closed by afternoon. Flowers late May through
early October.

Scarce in shrubland, woodland, and forest, goatsbeard
is quite common on medium and fine soils around lawns
and gardens below 8,000 feet elevation; it seems most abundant between 6,000 and 7,000 feet. Common associates are
prickly lettuce *(Senchus asper),* common dandelion *(Taraxacum officinale),* and small-flowered gaura *(Gaura parviflora).*

NAVAJO USES

Goatsbeard is an adventive (a recently introduced and thus
scarcely established species from Europe). It has no recognized Navajo use. Traditionally, Navajos use plants mentioned in the Navajo creation stories — plants native to the
reservation and given to the Navajos for their use.

REFERENCES

No recorded information.

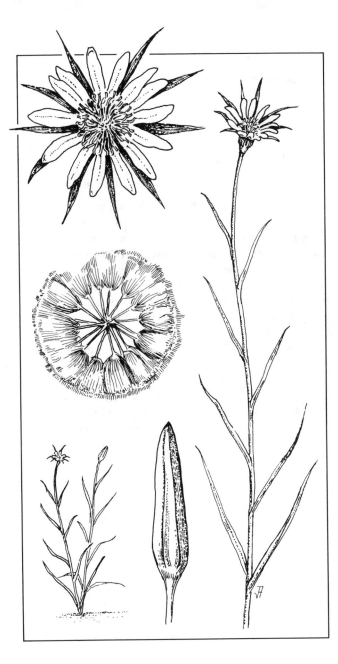

GOOSEBERRY *(Ribes)*
wild currant, squaw currant, waxcurrant

Ribes cereum (Dougl.) ('rye-beez 'see-ree-um)
Ribes: From the Latin word *ribas,* "a plant with sour sap"
cereum: From the Latin word *cera,* "waxy" (refers to the
    waxy fruit)

NAVAJO NAME: *K'íńjíł'ahí,* "skinned from a tree"

DESCRIPTION & DISTRIBUTION
Wax currant is a medium-sized shrub, 3 to 5 feet high, with
many main branches arising from its base. As the plant ages,
the stem color changes from tan to gray. The broad leaves
are neither conspicuously hairy nor waxy. Absence of
spines and presence of reddish fruits distinguish it from
most other Navajoland gooseberries *(Ribes* sp.). Flowers are
pinkish near the base and whitish beyond; they appear May
through early August.

    Wax currant occurs sparsely among Douglas fir *(Pseu-
dotsuga menziesii)* and Colorado blue spruce *(Picea pungens)*
up to 9,000 feet and in narrow canyons along streams down
to 5,500 feet. It is most common in ponderosa pine *(Pinus
ponderosa)* and Gambel oak *(Quercus gambelii)* forests at
elevations of about 7,500 feet. Close associates are other
gooseberries *(Ribes* sp.), Arizona rose *(Rosa arizonica),* snowberries *(Symphoricarpos* sp.), and bracken fern *(Pteridium
aquilinum).*

NAVAJO USES
CEREMONIAL: *K'íńjíł'ahí* is used in Evil Way, Night Way, and
Mountaintop Way ceremonies.
    MEDICINAL: Wax currant is used as a poultice for sores.
    OTHER: Navajos ate the fruit and leaves. The fruit could
be eaten raw, or cooked, or ground with cornmeal and
made into bread. The leaves were fried with fat.
    The hard wood was used to make arrow shafts and the
Navajo spining stick, *bee adizí.* The spindle is a smooth

42

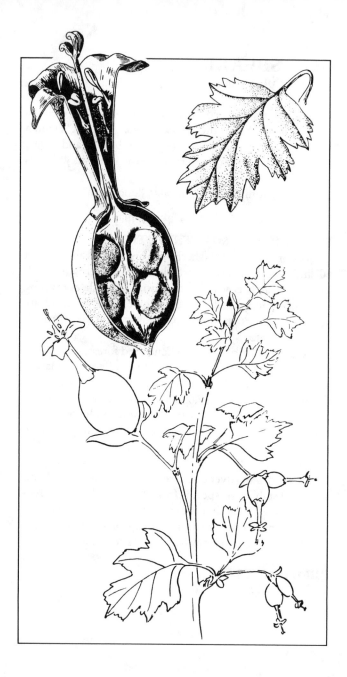

3-foot-long stick, pointed at both ends with a whorl (a 4- or 5-inch diameter circle with a small hole in the center) tightly stuck about 5 inches from one end. The stick is made of wax currant; the whorl is pine (Pinus sp.).

The weaver places the carded wool on the whorl and leans the spindle against her thigh. She rapidly rotates the spindle back and forth with one hand while gently pulling the wool into yarn with the other. A good Navajo weaver can turn roughly carded wool into a fine, tight yarn in one spinning.

REFERENCES

Elmore, Francis, *Ethnobotany of the Navajo*, 52.
Franciscan Fathers, *An Ethnologic Dictionary of the Navajo Language*, 199, 226, 243, 318–19.
Hocking, George M., "Some Plant Materials Used Medicinally and Otherwise by the Navaho Indians in the Chaco Canyon, New Mexico," *El Palacio*, 162–63.
Vestal, Paul A., *Ethnobotany of the Ramah Navajo*, 29.
Wyman, Leland, and Stuart Harris, *Ethnobotany of the Kayenta Navajo*, 26.
———, *Navajo Indian Medical Ethnobotany*, 29–30, 40.
Young, Stella, *Native Plants Used by the Navajo*, 21.

GOOSEFOOT *(Chenopodium)*
common lambsquarters, white goosefoot

Chenopodium album L. (kee-no-'poh-dee-um 'al-bum)
Chenopodium: Greek for "goosefoot," refers to the shape of the leaves
album: White

NAVAJO NAME: *Tłʼoh łigaii*, "grass white"

DESCRIPTION & DISTRIBUTION
Common lambsquarters is an erect, annual herb under 4 feet tall. Herbage is mealy but not hairy; stems may have lengthwise, red streaks. Small greenish flowers are open from mid-May through mid-October.

From about 8,000 feet down to the lowest elevations on the reservation (about 3,000 feet), this weed grows mostly on medium-textured, disturbed soils in depressions, along roads, around fields, and corrals. Associates are pigweeds (*Amaranthus* sp.), kochia (*Kochia* sp.), bassia (*Bassia* sp.), cocklebur (*Xanthium* sp.), golden crownbeard (*Verbesina encelioides),* and Russian thistle (*Salsola iberica*).

NAVAJO USES
Common lambsquarters was once a major food plant of the Navajos. Even as late as the 1940s, Navajos were known to have stored white goosefoot seeds for winter.

Dried plants were threshed on a blanket to winnow the seeds, ground lightly to loosen the perianth (the outer envelope of the flower), winnowed again, washed, dried, and finally ground with corn. They were thought to have a bitter taste if used alone.

The ground seeds make a light gray flour that can be used like corn meal: it can be made into a bread that is baked in ashes, made into dumplings that are boiled in water or goat's milk, or made into a mush.

Tender young plants are eaten raw or cooked with other foods. *See appendix, page 140, for nutritional composition.*

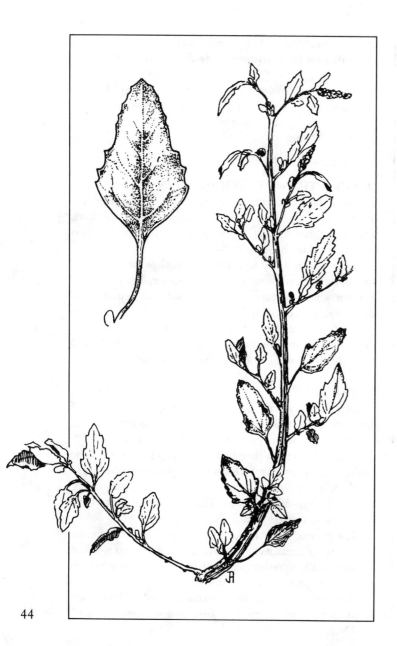

CEREMONIAL: *Tł'oh łigaii* is a ceremonial food in the Night Way. It is used to make equipment for other ceremonies.

REFERENCES

Elmore, Francis, *Ethnobotany of the Navajo,* 43–44.

Franciscan Fathers, *An Ethnologic Dictionary of the Navajo Language,* 185.

Hocking, George M., "Some Plant Materials Used Medicinally and Otherwise by the Navaho in the Chaco Canyon, New Mexico," *El Palacio,* 149.

Matthews, Washington, "Navajo Names for Plants," *The American Naturalist,* 768.

Watt, B. K., and A. L. Merrill, et al., *Composition of Foods, Agricultural Handbook No. 8,* 37.

Vestal, Paul A., *Ethnobotany of the Ramah Navajo,* 24–25.

Wyman, Leland, and Stuart Harris, *Navajo Indian Medical Ethnobotany,* 33, 38.

Young, Stella, *Native Plants Used by the Navajo,* 6.

GRAMA *(Bouteloua)*
blue grama

Bouteloua gracilis (H.B.K.) Lag. ex Steud. (boo-tuh-'loo-
    ah 'grass-il-iss)
Bouteloua: Named after Claudia Boutelou, a professor
             of agriculture at a university in Madrid,
             Spain
gracilis: Slender, graceful

NAVAJO NAME: *Tl'oh nástasí,* "bent grass"

DESCRIPTION & DISTRIBUTION

Sodgrass at lower elevations, bunchgrass at higher elevations, blue grama is a perennial grass seldom exceeding 2
feet in height. Comblike spikes or reduced flowers are
distinctive. Dormant most of the year, it grows from June
to November and flowers July through October.

More abundant than any other grass on the reservation,
blue grama ranges up to about 8,500 feet but is a subdomi-
nant only between 5,500 and 7,500 feet in blue grama,
galleta *(Hilaria jamesii),* sand dropseed *(Sporobolus cryptandrus),* and Indian ricegrass *(Oryzopsis hymenoides)* grassland;
fourwing saltbush *(Atriplex canescens),* shadscale *(Atriplex
confertifolia),* big rabbitbrush *(Chrysothamnus nauseosus),* and
broom snakeweed *(Gutierrezia sarothrae)* shrubland; Colorado pinyon *(Pinus edulis),* Utah juniper *(Juniperus osteosperma),* and oneseed juniper *(Juniperus monosperma)* woodland;
and ponderosa pine *(Pinus ponderosa),* Colorado pinyon
(Pinus edulis), and Gambel oak *(Quercus gambelii)* forest. Soil
textures of sites are usually coarse to medium.

NAVAJO USES

MEDICINAL: Blue grama can be used to heal cuts in humans
or animals by placing a chewed root on the wound. The
root is also used in life medicine (see yarrow). An antidote
for too much life medicine is made of a mixture of *Tl'oh*

nástasí and snakeweed (*Gutierrezia* sp.). The whole plant is made into a beverage for postpartum pain.

CEREMONIAL: Blue grama is used as blackening and charcoal in Evil Way and Enemy Way. It is also used for other ceremonial equipment such as the prayersticks in the Chiricahua Wind Way and the wand in the Enemy Way.

OTHER: Some people consider blue grama the most important forage grass on the Navajo Reservation. It is a major feed for horses, cattle, sheep, and goats.

REFERENCES

Elmore, Francis, *Ethnobotany of the Navajo*, 25.
Franciscan Fathers, *An Ethnologic Dictionary of the Navajo Language*, 366–69, 416–17.
Martin, Neils, *Common Range Plants*, 1.
Vestal, Paul A., *Ethnobotany of the Ramah Navajo*, 15–16.
Wyman, Leland, and Stuart Harris, *Navajo Indian Medical Ethnobotany*, 34, 36, 73–74.
Young, Stella, *Native Plants Used by the Navajo*, 70.

GREASEWOOD (*Sarcobatus*)
black greasewood

Sarcobatus vermiculatus (Hook.) Torr. (sar-koh-'bay-tuss verr-mih-kew-'lay-tuss)
Sarcobatus: Sarco, "fleshy," *batus*, Greek for "bramble bush"
vermiculatus: From the Latin *vermis*, for "worm," because the embryo of this plant has a "wormy" appearance

NAVAJO NAME: *Díwózhiishzhiin*, "black bushy shrub"

DESCRIPTION & DISTRIBUTION

Black greasewood is a thorny gray-green shrub resembling fourwing saltbush (*Atriplex canescens*) but is more open, less symmetrical, and usually taller (up to 7 feet) than the latter. Stems are whitish, then pale gray with darker markings, and finally darker gray. Leaves are linear, as long as 1½ inches, and fleshier than those of fourwing saltbush. The female shrubs bear fruits with a peripheral wing about ½ inch in diameter. Flowers July through early September.

Most common below 6,000 feet elevation, black greasewood occurs at elevations up to about 6,800 feet. In woodland and shrubland it dominates certain moist, saline soils, usually of medium or fine textures. Close associates are smaller saltbushes (*Atriplex* sp.), seepweeds (*Suaeda* sp.), saltgrass (*Distichlis* sp.), and Russian thistle (*Salsola iberica*).

NAVAJO USES

CEREMONIAL: *Díwózhiishzhiin* is used to make equipment for the Lightning Chant and the Mountain Chant.

MEDICINAL: Greasewood is chewed and applied to the stings of ants, wasps, and bees. It is also used in childbirth.

OTHER: One of the best-known uses of black greasewood is for *ádístsiin*, or "mush sticks." They are used to stir mush in certain ceremonies like *kinaaldá*, the girls' puberty ritual, and Navajo weddings. *See appendix, page 141, for description of* ádístsiin *ritual.*

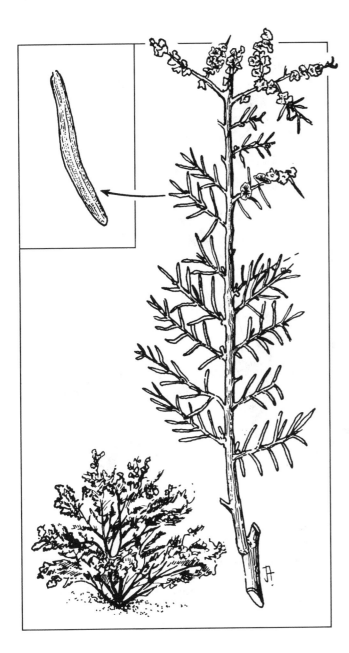

Because greasewood is hard, it is used for other household equipment: Navajo dice, knitting needles, heald sticks, war bows, and bird snares. The corn planting stick and the awls used in making lightning mats (see cattail) are made of greasewood.

Black greasewood is used in making red, yellow, and blue dyes.

Greasewood burns like oak; its ashes remain hot for a long time and can be used to cook food. It is also used for firewood pokers, as the shaft in the fire drill, and to burn out cottonwood when making wooden boxes from logs or burls.

Because the plants are tall, they provide forage for sheep when it snows.

The Navajo once ate greasewood seeds.

REFERENCES

Elmore, Francis, *Ethnobotany of the Navajo*, 44–45.

Franciscan Fathers, *An Ethnologic Dictionary of the Navajo Language*, 116–17, 185, 218, 220, 243, 318–19.

Hocking, George M., "Some Plant Materials Used Medicinally and Otherwise by the Navaho Indians in the Chaco Canyon, New Mexico," *El Palacio*, 155.

Kluckhohn, Clyde, et al., *Navajo Material Culture*, 124–25, 416–17.

Vestal, Paul A., *Ethnobotany of the Ramah Navajo*, 25.

Wyman, Leland, and Stuart Harris, *Navajo Indian Medical Ethnobotany*, 26, 39.

Young, Stella, *Native Plants Used by the Navajo*, 77, 105.

GROUNDSEL *(Senecio)*
threadleaf groundsel

Senecio douglasii DC. (sen-'nee-see-oh 'dugluss-eye)

Senecio: From the Latin *senex,* "old man"; refers to the
       whitish hairs of many species, including this one

douglasii: Named for the Scottish botanist David
       Douglas (1798–1834), who collected for the
       Royal Horticultural Society of London and
       discovered the species

NAVAJO NAME: *Azee' háářdzid,* "rotten medicine"

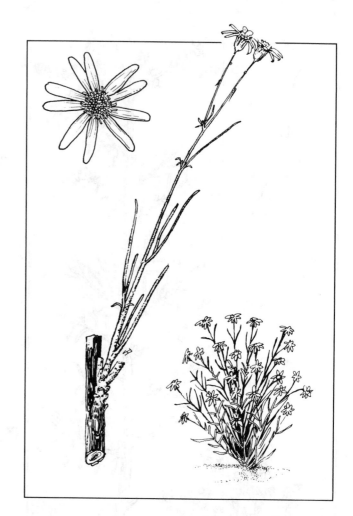

DESCRIPTION & DISTRIBUTION

Threadleaf groundsel is a subshrub with many stems forming a clump up to about 3 feet tall. Stems are woody and
beige only a few inches above ground; higher they are
greenish but covered with a dense, loose mat of white
cobwebby hairs. Leaves also appear whitish due to the hairs.
The plant closely resembles manyheaded ragwort *(Senecio
multicapitatus),* but the latter has more and smaller flower
heads and lacks the cobwebby mat over its dark green herbage. Flowers (yellow rays with an orange disk) bloom May
through October.

    The elevational range of threadleaf groundsel is be-
tween 4,000 and 7,000 feet. The sites are gravelly roadsides,
slopes, and wash margins, where it grows in association
with Rocky Mountain beeplant *(Cleome serrulata),* sandhill
muhly *(Muhlenbergia pungens),* bottlebrush *(Sitanion hystrix),*
squirreltail *(Sitanion jubatum),* and needle-and-thread *(Stipa
comata).*

NAVAJO USES

MEDICINAL: *Azee' háářdzid* is used as a medicine for arthritis,
rheumatism, and boils. The medicine may be drunk or used
as a poultice. Another treatment is to boil the plant and ex-
pose the sore of the patient to the steam.

REFERENCES

Hocking, George M., "Some Plant Materials Used
    Medicinally and Otherwise by the Navaho Indians in
    the Chaco Canyon, New Mexico," *El Palacio,* 156.

Wyman, Leland, and Stuart Harris, *Ethnobotany of the
    Kayenta Navajo,* 49.

———— , *Navajo Indian Medical Ethnobotany,* 58–59.

GUMWEED *(Grindelia)*
rayless gumweed

Grindelia aphanactis Rydb. (grin-'del-ee-uh af-an-'ak-tuss)
Grindelia: Named for D. H. Grindel, (1766–1836),
    German professor of botany at Riga
aphanactis: From the Greek *aphan,* from *aphanes,* "invis-
    ible," "secret," "unknown"; and *aktinos,* a "ray"
    or "beam" (the plant lacks rays)

NAVAJO NAME: *Wóláchíí' beeyigá,* "red ant killer"

DESCRIPTION & DISTRIBUTION

Rayless gumweed is an erect, herbaceous biennial usually
with only 1 main stem up to 1½ feet tall. Leaves are as long
as 2 inches and are toothed along margins. Stem color varies
from purple at the top of the plant to pale green at the base.
Heads have a gold rim and a brown center. Flowers late June
through August.

    Elevations between 5,000 and 6,500 feet, and soils of
medium texture in depressions, rills, and around irrigated
fields are sites for rayless gumweed. Associates include the
sunflowers (*Helianthus* sp.), common cocklebur *(Xanthium
strumarium),* and the sweet clovers (*Melilotus* sp.). Rayless
gumweed occurs, with other associates, up to almost 7,000
feet and down to the lower points of the reservation.

NAVAJO USES

MEDICINAL: Rayless gumweed is an emetic and diuretic
used to treat venereal disease and urinary problems. It is
also used internally and externally to treat sickness or bites
caused by red ants. The sticky juice can hold cuts together
until they heal.

    CEREMONIAL: *Wóláchíí' beeyigá* may be included in the
medicine for Red Ant Way, Beauty Way, or Plume Way.

    OTHER: A strong mixture of rayless gumweed and water
is poured on an ant hill to kill the ants.

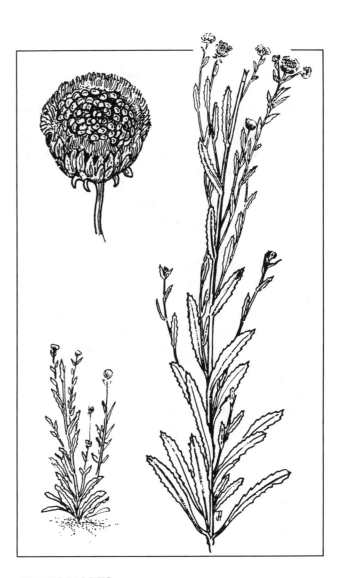

REFERENCES

Vestal, Paul A., *Ethnobotany of the Ramah Navajo,* 51.
Wyman, Leland, and Stuart Harris, *Navajo Indian Medical
    Ethnobotany,* 24, 34, 47, 60–61, 65.

HERON BILL *(Erodium)*
redstem filaree, crane's bill, red stem, alfilaria

Erodium cicutarium (L.) L'Her. (ee-'rok-dee-um sik-kyew-'tay-ree-um)

Erodium: From the Greek *erodios,* "heron." After the corolla falls, the style and ovaries of *Erodium* sp. look like the head of a heron.

cicutarium: Named for water hemlock (*Cicuta* sp.), which it is said to resemble

NAVAJO NAME: *Tsís'nádą́ą́,* "bee food"; and *Chooyin azee',* "menstruation medicine"

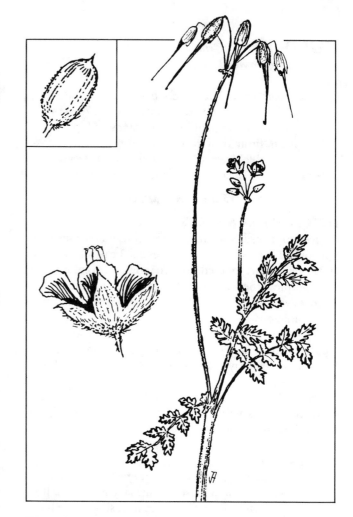

DESCRIPTION & DISTRIBUTION

Redstem filaree is an annual herb with small, pinkish to lavender flowers and prostrate to semierect stems ascending a few inches above ground. Leaves are divided into several parts, which in turn are deeply cut. The fruit has a long, slender beak, which buries it and its seeds in the soil by coiling and relaxing as it is dried and moistened. Successive generations flower from February through early November.

Ranging from the lowest elevations on the reservation upward to about 7,800 feet, redstem filaree is a member of many communities of plants in disturbed areas of medium to fine soils along roadsides, in depressions, campgrounds, and in clearings in shrubland, woodland, and forests.

NAVAJO USES

MEDICINAL: Redstem filaree is used to treat excessive menstruation. It is also used for wildcat, bobcat, or mountain lion bites.

CEREMONIAL: *Tsis'nádą́ą́* is used on prayersticks and as medicine in many ceremonies.

OTHER: The Navajo consider *Erodium cicutarium* a new plant, although it was introduced fairly early by the Spaniards. Sheep eat redstem filaree in early spring.

REFERENCES

Elmore, Francis, *Ethnobotany of the Navajo,* 59.

Franciscan Fathers, *An Ethnologic Dictionary of the Navajo Language,* 189.

Vestal, Paul A., *Ethnobotany of the Ramah Navajo,* 34.

Wyman, Leland, and Stuart Harris, *Ethnobotany of the Kayenta Navajo,* 29, 62.

HOREHOUND *(Marrubium)*
common horehound

Marrubium vulgare L. (mar-'roo-bee-um vul-'gay-ree)
Marrubium: From the Hebrew *marrob,* "bitter juice"
vulgare: From the Latin *vulgaris,* "common"

NAVAJO NAME: *Azee' nidoot'eezhii łibáhígíí,* "gray knotted medicine"

DESCRIPTION & DISTRIBUTION

Common horehound is a perennial herb with many stems arising erectly from the root crown to a height of about 2 feet. Stems are thick and yellowish under a dense covering of cobwebby hairs. The thick, green leaves have sunken veins, and a dense, cobwebby layer of whitish hairs; length seldom exceeds 1 inch. Tiny, whitish flowers are tightly clustered in the angles of the stems and the leaf pairs. Flowers June through early September.

Scattered, often isolated, stands of common horehound grow in depressions of medium to fine soils at elevations below 7,000 feet. The plant is not common.

NAVAJO USES

MEDICINAL: Common horehound is used to treat a variety of illnesses. The plant is soaked in water, and the resulting liquid is used to treat indigestion, stomachache, influenza, lameness, colds, coughs, sore throat, and general aches and pains. It is thought to be an effective treatment for diarrhea and dysentery in young children.

It is used in childbirth.

CEREMONIAL: *Azee' nidoot'eezhii łibáhígíí* is one of the plants used as medicine in the Shooting Way, Navajo Wind Way, and in ceremonies that treat lung disease and fever.

It is aromatic, as are most of the plants in the Lamiaceae (mint) family. Most medicines used in Navajo ceremonies include an aromatic plant, many from this plant family. The medicine is first applied ceremonially to the patient's body, then given to the patient to drink.

HOUSEHOLD: Common horehound is eaten by livestock, but people say it gives mutton and goat meat a bitter flavor.

REFERENCES

Elmore, Francis, *Ethnobotany of the Navajo,* 73.
Vestal, Paul A., *Ethnobotany of the Ramah Navajo,* 41.
Wyman, Leland, and Stuart Harris, *Navajo Indian Medical Ethnobotany,* 20, 24, 45, 55–57, 66–67, 69.

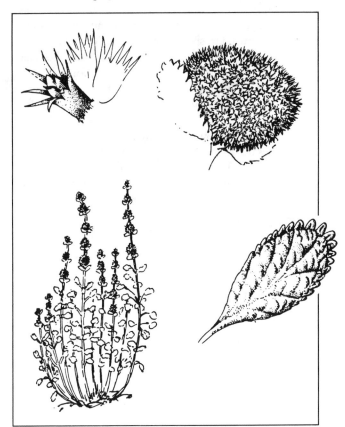

HORSETAIL *(Equisetum)*
common horsetail, common scouring-rush

Equisetum hiemale L. (ek-wi-'see-tum hi-ee-'ma-lee)
Equisetum: From *equus,* "horse" and *setus,* "bristle" or "tail"
hiemale: "of winter;" often referring to evergreen plants

NAVAJO NAME: *Ałtį́į́' jik'aashí,* "bow smoother"

DESCRIPTION & DISTRIBUTION

Common scouring-rush is an erect perennial herb of unusual appearance. It may reach 3 feet tall, but 2½ feet may be average. Stems are dull green and seem leafless; leaves are reduced to sheaths around the joints. There are no flowers or seeds, but spores are produced in a conelike structure terminating the stem. It resembles only its close relatives, meadow horsetail *(Equisetum arvense)* and smooth horsetail *(Equisetum laevigatum)*; it is a horsetail, not a rush *(Juncus* sp.).

This horsetail grows along streams, washes, and irrigation ditches below about 7,000 feet elevation. Scarce above 6,000 feet, it is often at lower elevations with common reed *(Phragmites communis),* meadow horsetail *(Equisetum arvense),* rushes *(Juncus* sp.), sedges *(Carex* sp.), inland saltgrass *(Distichlis stricta),* and other grasses (Poaceae sp.) on coarse, saturated soils in canyons and valleys.

NAVAJO USES

MEDICINAL: Horsetail is said to be used for a variety of internal ailments such as stomach problems and nausea. It may be used for skin problems and bites of venomous animals.

CEREMONIAL: *Ałtį́į́' jik'aashí* is one of the plants used as an emetic in five- and nine-night ceremonies.

REFERENCES

Wyman, Leland, and Stuart Harris, *Navajo Indian Medical Ethnobotany,* 57–58.

52

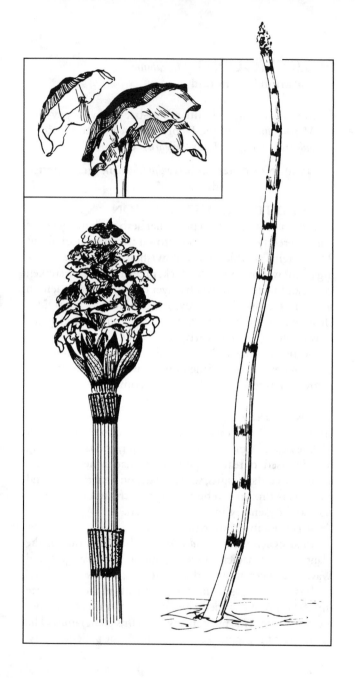

IRIS *(Iris)*
Rocky Mountain iris, western wild iris, western blue flag, fleur-de-lis

Iris missouriensis Nutt. ('eye-riss mih-'zoo-ri-en-siss)
Iris: From the Greek *iridos,* "rainbow," because of the
   many colors of the flowers
missouriensis: Of or from Missouri

NAVAJO NAME: *Niteel bit'ąą'łanígíí,* "many leaved
   broad plant"

DESCRIPTION & DISTRIBUTION
Rocky Mountain iris is an erect, perennial herb with
rhizomes, long gray-green leaves, leafless flowering stems,
and pale blue and white flowers with purplish veins. Height
is under 2 feet. Leaves are about ½ inch wide. Flowers late
May through early July.

Mountain meadows and marshes at about 8,000 feet
elevation are typical habitats. Dense stands may exclude
most other plants except grasses.

NAVAJO USES
CEREMONIAL: *Niteel bit'ąą'łanígíí* is used as a Holy Way and
Lightning Way emetic.

HOUSEHOLD: Rocky Mountain iris makes a green dye.

REFERENCES
Elmore, Francis, *Ethnobotany of the Navajo,* 37.
Franciscan Fathers, *An Ethnologic Dictionary of the Navajo
   Language,* 191.
Vestal, Paul A., *Ethnobotany of the Ramah Navajo,* 21.
Wyman, Leland, and Stuart Harris, *Navajo Indian Medical
   Ethnobotany,* 32, 37, 57–58.

JOINT-FIR *(Ephedra)*
Torrey joint-fir, Torrey Mormon tea

Ephedra torreyana S. Wats. (eh-'feh-druh 'torrey-ay-nuh)
Ephedra: Greek for "horsetail"
torreyana: Named for Dr. John Torrey (1796–1873),
           a medical doctor and Professor Emeritus of
           botany and chemistry at the New York Col-
           lege of Physicians and Surgeons. He iden-
           tified many plants for John C. Fremont.

NAVAJO NAME: *Tł'oh azihii łibáhígíí,* "gray rubbing grass"

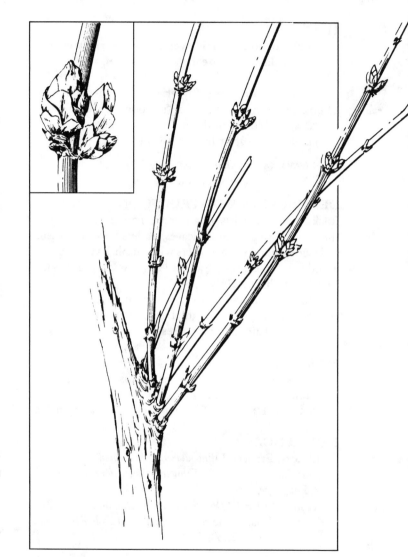

DESCRIPTION & DISTRIBUTION

Torrey joint-fir is a shrubby, densely branched plant with a woody stem base. Its height seldom exceeds 2 feet. Stems are olive green to blue-green and furrowed lengthwise. Leaves have been reduced to short scales, 3 at each joint. There are no showy flowers or fruits; on female plants, seeds are borne within the scales of soft cones. Another local joint-fir, green joint-fir *(Ephedra viridis)*, is similar, but its color is yellow-green, it has only 2 scale leaves per joint, and it grows from low areas into mountains.

Below about 6,000 feet, Torrey joint-fir is scattered in saltbush *(Atriplex* sp.) shrubland (5,000 to 6,000 feet) but is one of the dominants of the community of blackbrush *(Coleogyne ramosissima),* saltbush *(Atriplex* sp.), and joint-fir at lower elevations of Navajoland. It usually occupies hummocks or small dunes of coarse soil that it holds against erosion.

NAVAJO USES

MEDICINAL: *Tł'oh azihii łibáhígíí* is a diuretic used to treat bladder and kidney problems. It is also considered an effective treatment for venereal disease and afterbirth pains.

OTHER: As the common name implies, Mormon tea was used as a hot drink by pioneers in the West. Navajos roast the branches before boiling them in water to take away the plant's bitter taste.

54

REFERENCES
Elmore, Francis, *Ethnobotany of the Navajo,* 24.
Wyman, Leland, and Stuart Harris, *Navajo Indian Medical Ethnobotany,* 33, 36, 60–62.

JUNIPER *(Juniperus)*
Utah juniper, desert juniper

Juniperus osteosperma (Torr.) Little (jew-'nip-er-us
    os-tee-oh-'sper-muh)
Juniperus: Name given to the genus by Virgil from the
    Celtic word *juniperus,* which means "rough"
osteosperma: "Bone-seed"; from the Greek *osteon,*
    "bone," and *sperma,* "seed"

NAVAJO NAME: *Gad biką'ígíí,* "male juniper"

DESCRIPTION & DISTRIBUTION

Utah juniper is usually a small evergreen tree up to about 25 feet high. Occasionally it is shrublike and then is almost indistinguishable from oneseed juniper *(Juniperus monosperma).* All members of the species have round, bluish, fleshy cones, whereas the population of oneseed juniper consists of male trees and female trees with only the latter bearing the so-called berries.

Between elevations of about 4,500 to 7,000 feet, Utah juniper occurs in shrubland, woodland, and forest. In the saltbush *(Atriplex* sp.) shrublands (about 4,500 to 5,500 feet), it is scattered on the flats but grows in denser stands on ridges.

With Colorado pinyon *(Pinus edulis),* it dominates the conifer woodland (5,500 to 7,000 feet) and displaces pinyon on south slopes and other marginal sites. Where woodland and forest overlap (about 6,800 to 7,200 feet on east or west mountain sides), this juniper is scarce and inconspicuous among ponderosa pine *(Pinus ponderosa),* and Rocky Mountain juniper *(Juniperus scopulorum).*

NAVAJO USES

MEDICINAL: Juniper serves a variety of medicinal purposes, from an emetic to a medicine for headaches, influenza, stomachaches, nausea, acne, spider bites, and postpartum pain.

One of its most comforting uses is as a hot water bottle: A heated branch wrapped in a slightly damp cloth is placed on an aching ear, arm or leg, or on the abdomen of a woman in labor.

CEREMONIAL: *Gad biką'ígíí* is used as an emetic in the five- and nine-night sings and for many ceremonial items.

OTHER: Juniper berries can be eaten in the fall when they are ripe. Mothers put bracelets of dried juniper berries, called ghost beads, on their babies when they go to bed to keep them from having bad dreams.

Juniper burns with a hot flame and clear smoke so it is the preferred wood for cooking. Its straight branches are used to build summer shelters, fences, corrals, and hogan roofs.

Documented uses of *Gad bika'ígíí* are as diverse as any plant's: cradleboard canopy, good luck token (it has been reported several times that juniper needles are chewed, then spit out for good luck, as in the face of a balky burro), and as a necessary ingredient in cooking traditional foods.

Juniper ash water serves as baking powder and flavoring for corn dishes; it adds traces of iron, zinc, calcium, and potassium to food. *(See appendix, page 141, for ash water, Blue Corn Bread, and Juniper Wool and Buckskin Dye recipes.)*

According to Navajo legends, juniper was important in the development of the Navajo wedding basket.

In the early days, a Navajo woman sitting under a tree weaving a basket wondered how to finish the rim. Just then, Coyote tossed a small juniper branch into her lap. The woman realized that she could make a beautiful basket by imitating the pattern of the juniper leaves.

To this day, Navajo baskets, especially Navajo wedding baskets, have a rim that looks like the pattern of juniper leaves.

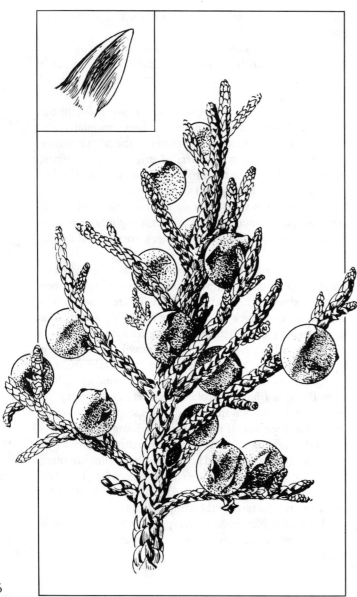

REFERENCES

Bailey, Flora, "Navajo Foods and Cooking Methods," *American Anthropologist*, 277–78, 280–81.

Elmore, Francis, *Ethnobotany of the Navajo*, 17–19.

Franciscan Fathers, *An Ethnologic Dictionary of the Navajo Language*, 31, 66–67, 190, 233, 242, 257, 336, 368, 371–72.

Hocking, George M., "Some Plant Materials Used Medicinally and Otherwise by the Navaho Indians in the Chaco Canyon, New Mexico," *El Palacio*, 152, 161.

Wyman, Leland, and Stuart Harris, *Navajo Indian Medical Ethnobotany*, 26, 36, 57–58, 62–63, 73–74.

Young, Stella, *Native Plants Used by the Navajo*, 36, 41, 48, 77, 88, 101, 106–107.

Rocky Mountain juniper,
Rocky Mountain cedar, cedro

Juniperus scopulorum Sarg. (jew-'nip-er-us
    scop-yew-'loh-rum)
scopulorum: Of rocky places

NAVAJO NAME: *Gad ni'eełii,* "drooping juniper"

DESCRIPTION & DISTRIBUTION

Rocky Mountain juniper is an evergreen tree growing up
to 30 feet tall. It resembles Utah juniper *(Juniperus osteosperma),* but its older bark is more scaly than shreddy, and its
branchlets are flattened and drooping. Foliage is yellow-
green; branches are olive, becoming pale brown, brown,
then gray-brown with age (oldest bark also is gray-brown).
The so-called berries are small, about ¼ inch across, and
violet under a coating of gray wax.

Although ranging from almost 9,000 feet on south-
facing mountainsides down to about 6,500 feet in rocky
canyons, Rocky Mountain juniper is most abundant at
about 7,000 feet in overlapping pinyon-juniper *(Pinus edulis*
and *Juniperus osteosperma)* woodlands and pine-oak *(Pinus
ponderosa* and *Quercus gambelii)* forests. Its most frequent
associate may be Gambel oak *(Quercus gambelii).*

NAVAJO USES

MEDICINAL: To remove dandruff, Rocky Mountain juniper
and a grass, probably cheatgrass *(Bromus tectorum),* are
rubbed into the scalp after the hair is washed. The needles
are made into a tea to treat pain, stomach troubles, diarrhea, and spider bites.

CEREMONIAL: *Gad ni'eełii* is used for medicine and for
ceremonial equipment in the Blessing Way, Evil Way, and
other ceremonies.

OTHER: A sprig of Rocky Mountain juniper is carried
at night for protection against witches, ghosts, or evil
spirits.

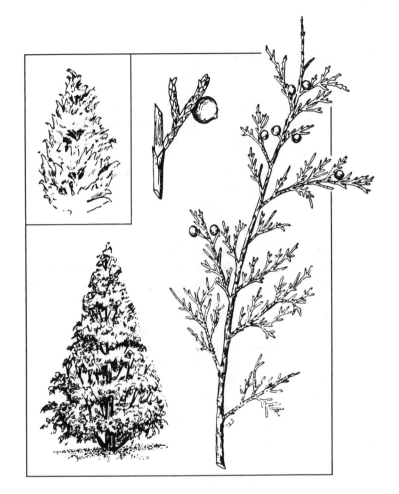

REFERENCES

Elmore, Francis, *Ethnobotany of the Navajo,* 20.
Matthews, Washington, "Navajo Names for Plants," *The
    American Naturalist,* 776.
Wyman, Leland, and Stuart Harris, *Ethnobotany of the
    Kayenta Navajo,* 15, 61.
———, *Navajo Indian Medical Ethnobotany,* 26, 36, 74.
Young, Stella, *Native Plants Used by the Navajo,* 89, 101,
    107.

LARKSPUR *(Delphinium)*
Nelson larkspur, wild larkspur

Delphinium nelsoni Greene (del-'fin-ee-um 'nel-sun-eye)
Delphinium: Dolphin (refers to the shape of the nectar-
              containing organ)
nelsoni: Named for Aven Nelson, twentieth-century
           Rocky Mountain botanist, professor of botany,
           and curator of the herbarium of the University
           of Wyoming

NAVAJO NAME: *Tádídíín dootł'izh,* "blue pollen"

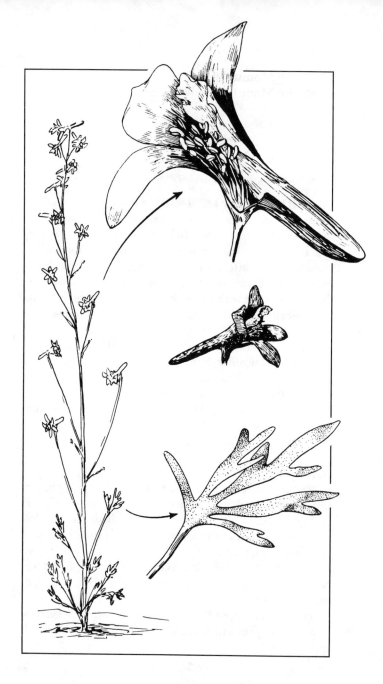

DESCRIPTION & DISTRIBUTION

Nelson larkspur is an erect, herbaceous perennial up to 15
inches tall. The main stem seldom branches, has a cluster
of leaves at its base, and a few leaves scattered along its
length up to the white and blue flowers. It resembles
barestem larkspur *(Delphinium scaposum),* which grows at
lower elevations. Flowers May through June.

    Widely but sparsely distributed throughout forests of
ponderosa pine *(Pinus ponderosa)* and Gambel oak *(Quercus
gambelii),* it may also range down to 6,500 feet in pinyon-
juniper *(Pinus edulis* and *Juniperus* sp.) woodlands and up to
8,500 feet in the spruce-fir *(Picea engelmannii* and *Abies
lasiocarpa)* forests.

NAVAJO USES

CEREMONIAL: The blue petals of *tádídíín dootł'izh* are ground
with other plants and used for sacred pollen. Blue is the
sacred color of the south.

REFERENCES

    Elmore, Francis, *Ethnobotany of the Navajo,* 47.
    Vestal, Paul A., *Ethnobotany of the Ramah Navajo,* 27.
    Wyman, Leland, and Stuart Harris, *Navajo Indian Medical
        Ethnobotany,* 32, 39, 71.

LOCO WEED *(Astragalus)*
spotted loco, blue loco

Astragalus lentiginosus Dougl. ex Hook. (ass-'trag-al-us
len-tih-gih-'no-sus)
Astragalus: A bone; from the Greek *astragalos,* "of the
ankle joint"
lentiginosus: Freckles; from the Latin *lentigo,* "freckles,"
which came from *len,* meaning "lentils"
(a type of bean)

NAVAJO NAME: *Dibéhaich'iidii,* "gray sheep scratch"

DESCRIPTION & DISTRIBUTION

Blue loco is an herbaceous biennial so variable in form and
color that it resembles many other locos (*Astragalus* sp.) and
crazyweeds (*Oxytropis* sp.). Stems are seldom erect; they
either lie on the ground but turn up at the ends, or they
rise obliquely. Height is under 1 foot, but stems may extend 2 feet in length. Young stems are green; they become
purplish with age. Flowers are blue and white. Pods are
yellow to green and are purple-blotched. Flowers April
through May.

Below elevations of about 6,000 feet, blue loco is scattered in woodland, shrubland, and desert, often along roads
or trails.

NAVAJO USES

MEDICINAL: Blue loco is one of the life medicines (see yarrow). It is a diuretic and is used for venereal disease and
stomach disorders. The crushed leaves are used to sooth
a bad back.

CEREMONIAL: *Dibéhaich'iidii* is a Bead Way medicine.

REFERENCES
Vestal, Paul A., *Ethnobotany of the Ramah Navajo,* 32.
Wyman, Leland, and Stuart Harris, *Ethnobotany of the
Kayenta Navajo,* 27.

LUPINE *(Lupinus)*
silvery lupine

Lupinus argenteus (Pursh) (loo-'pye-nus are-'jen-teh-us)
Lupinus: Wolf; implying that the plant tends to
    impoverish the soil
argenteus: Silvery; refers to the appearance of the leaves

NAVAJO NAME: *Azee' bíní'í,* "wondering about medicine"

DESCRIPTION & DISTRIBUTION
Silvery lupine is a perennial herb growing as tall as 2½ feet
from a woody root crown. The compound leaf has several
leaflets. Flowers are grayish lavender-blue. The fruit is a
special pod that splits open along two seams (most podlike
fruits split along one seam) to release the seeds at maturity.

This is a fairly common lupine in ponderosa pine *(Pinus
ponderosa)* and Gambel oak *(Quercus gambelii)* forests between elevations of 7,000 and 8,000 feet.

NAVAJO USES
MEDICINAL: A lotion made of the leaves of *Lupinus argenteus*
is used to treat poison ivy blisters.

CEREMONIAL: *Azee' bíní'í* is used in the Male Shooting
Way and Evil Way ceremonies.

REFERENCES
Franciscan Fathers, *An Ethnologic Dictionary of the Navajo
    Language,* 192, 409.
Vestal, Paul A., *Ethnobotany of the Ramah Navajo,* 32.
Young, Stella, *Native Plants Used by the Navajo,* 81.

MALLOW *(Malva)*
roundleaf mallow, cheeseweed mallow

Malva neglecta Wallr. ('mal-vuh neg-'lekt-uh)
Malva: From the Greek word for softening because
    of this genus' emollient qualities
neglecta: From the Latin *neg,* "not," and *legere,* "choose";
    now means "disregarded" or "of little value"

NAVAJO NAME: *Azee' bílátah łigaii,* "white-flowered
    medicine"

DESCRIPTION & DISTRIBUTION
Roundleaf mallow is a short, sparsely hairy, dull green biennial, herbaceous weed with semiprostrate to ascending
stems (as long as 1 foot), bearing roundish leaves and
medium-sized, white (tinged lavender) flowers. Height
seldom exceeds 6 inches. It is the only cheeseweed mallow
on the reservation. Flowers early May through early
October.

With other weeds, roundleaf mallow grows around
lawns, fields, gardens, and corrals on soils of medium to
fine texture at elevations below 7,750 feet.

NAVAJO USES
MEDICINAL: Roundleaf mallow is used as a lotion or internal medication for an injury or swelling.

REFERENCES
Vestal, Paul A., *Ethnobotany of the Ramah Navajo,* 36.

MANZANITA *(Arctostaphylos)*
greenleaf manzanita

Arctostaphylos patula Greene (ark-to-'staff-il-oss
  'pat-yew-luh)
Arctostaphylos: From the Greek *arktos,* "bear," and
  staphylo, "a grape cluster." Animals feed on
  the clustered fruit.
patula: "slightly spreading," "broad," "wide"

NAVAJO NAME: *Dinastsoh,* "big berry plant"

DESCRIPTION & DISTRIBUTION

Greenleaf manzanita is a small, spreading, prolifically branching shrub up to 3 feet tall. It resembles pointleaf manzanita *(Arctostaphylos pungens)*, and many Navajoland
specimens exhibit characteristics between the two. Pinkish
flowers May through June.

Dense thickets of greenleaf manzanita occur at about
8,500 feet on south slopes of some mountains with
ponderosa pine *(Pinus ponderosa)* and sagebrush *(Artemisia*
sp.) bushes. Distribution seems to be limited.

NAVAJO USES

MEDICINAL: Greenleaf manzanita is an emetic used to treat
stomach problems, bug and insect bites.

CEREMONIAL: *Dinastsoh* is one of the many plants used
as ceremonial emetics. It is also a ceremonial tobacco,
smoked by itself or with other plants.

OTHER: The fruits are eaten raw.

REFERENCES

Wyman, Leland, and Stuart Harris, *Ethnobotany of the
  Kayenta Navajo,* 35.
——— , *Navajo Indian Medical Ethnobotany,* 57, 58.

MAPLE *(Acer)*
inland box elder, ash-leaved elder

Acer negundo L. ('ay-ser neh-'gun-doh)

Acer: Maple tree. A suggested origin of *acer* is "sharp," "pointed," or "cutting," in reference to the hardness and firmness of the wood, which the Romans used for spears.

negundo: From the Dravidian language of India, Ceylon, and West Pakistan for the Old World box elder, *Vitex negundo*

NAVAJO NAME: *Sóól,* "the box elder"

DESCRIPTION & DISTRIBUTION

Inland box elder is a medium sized tree sometimes exceeding 30 feet in height. The crown is quite dense with soft, dull green foliage. The compound leaves are paired (opposite) at the joints of the young stems. Stems are smooth and green, then tan, then grayish brown as they age. Greenish flowers with petals open April through May.

Scattered within rocky washes and canyons below 7,500 feet, inland box elder does not associate with the closely related Rocky Mountain maple *(Acer glabrum)* of the higher mountainsides, but rather mingles with Gambel oak *(Quercus gambelii)* and shrubs on talus slopes (rock slides).

NAVAJO USES

CEREMONIAL: *Sóól* is used to make the prayersticks in the Mountain Way.

OTHER: In the old days, wooden bellows used in silversmithing and horseshoeing were made from *Sóól*. It is a good firewood.

REFERENCES

Elmore, Francis, *Ethnobotany of the Navajo,* 62.

Wyman, Leland, and Stuart Harris, *Ethnobotany of the Kayenta Navajo,* 31.

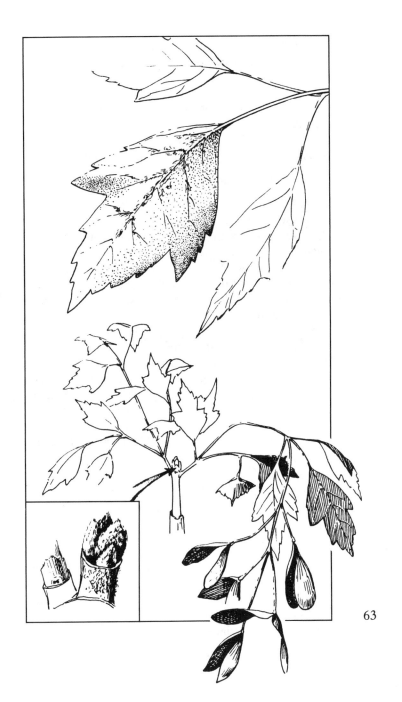

63

MARIPOSA *(Calochortus)*
golden mariposa, golden sego lily, nuttall sego lily, nuttall mariposa tulip

Calochortus aureus S. Wats (kal-lok-'kor-tus 'aw-ree-us)
Calochortus: From the Greek *kalos,* "beautiful," and
           chortos, "grass"
aureus: Golden; from the Latin *aurum,* "gold"

NAVAJO NAME: *Áłchínídą́ą́,* "children's food"

DESCRIPTION & DISTRIBUTION
Golden sego lily is an attractive perennial herb with a few
linear leaves on a stem arising from a bulb (subterranean
bud with roots) and bearing 1 or a few showy yellow
flowers. Its height is usually less than 15 inches. The fruit
is a capsule (dry at maturity and separating into 3 parts,
which then split open to release many small seeds). Flowers
April through June.

From about 5,000 feet up to 8,000 feet on soils of coarse
to medium textures, this sego lily is conspicuous but
scattered—never forming dense patches—in shrublands of
Torrey joint-fir *(Ephedra torreyana)* and spiny saltbush
(Atriplex confertifolia), and of big sagebrush *(Artemisia tridentata)* and fourwing saltbush *(Atriplex canescens);* in
woodlands of Colorado pinyon *(Pinus edulis),* oneseed
juniper *(Juniperus monosperma),* and Utah juniper *(Juniperus
osteosperma);* and in forests of ponderosa pine *(Pinus
ponderosa)* and Gambel oak *(Quercus gambelii).* Frequently,
its associates are wild onions *(Allium* sp.), wild relatives of
the carrot *(Apiaceae* sp.), foothill death-camas *(Zigadenus
paniculatus),* and larkspurs *(Delphinium* sp.).

NAVAJO USES
MEDICINAL: The bulb of *Áłchínídą́ą́* is a life medicine (see
yarrow).

OTHER: Golden sego lily bulbs were once a favorite
children's food. The bulbs were dug before the plant
bloomed in the spring, peeled, and eaten raw.

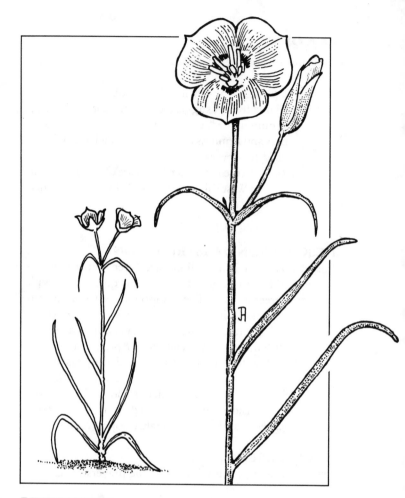

REFERENCES
Elmore, Francis, *Ethnobotany of the Navajo,* 32.
Matthews, Washington, "Navajo Names for Plants," *The
    American Naturalist,* 777.
Vestal, Paul A., *Ethnobotany of the Ramah Navajo,* 20.
Wyman, Leland, and Stuart Harris, *Navajo Indian Medical
    Ethnobotany,* 28.
———— , *Ethnobotany of the Kayenta Navajo,* 17.
Young, Stella, *Native Plants Used by the Navajo,* 8.

MILKWEED *(Asclepias)*

whorled milkweed, poison milkweed, horsetail milkweed, verticillata milkweed, verticillata silkweed

Asclepias subverticillata (Gray) Vail (as-'klee-pe-as sub-ver-tis-il-'lay-tuh)

Asclepias: From Greek mythology; Asklepios, the son of Apollo and Coronis, was also the god of medicine

subverticillata: sub, "somewhat," *verticillata,* "arranged in a whorl" (a circle or ring of organs, especially a leaf arrangement where three or more rise from the same node, or point on the stem)

NAVAJO NAME: *Ch'il'abe'éts'óóz,* "slender milky plant"

DESCRIPTION & DISTRIBUTION

Poison milkweed is an erect, dull green, herbaceous perennial growing from rhizomes, usually under 2 feet high. Leaves are slender and 3 or more inches long; they occur in groups of at least 3. Flowers are small and whitish, turning purple with age, and are clustered. Flowers June through August.

This milkweed ranges up to 7,750 feet and is the only local one that occurs on dry rangelands. (Its particular sites, however, are more moist than the general areas.) Evidently it adapts to any soil texture in depressions, rills, and washes and along roadsides where it associates with Rocky Mountain beeplant *(Cleome serrulata)* and Texas doveweed *(Croton texensis),* but patches are scattered. Stands of greatest density and extent grow in and around cultivated, irrigated fields, where it associates with common cocklebur *(Xanthium* sp.) and Russian knapweed *(Centaurea repens).*

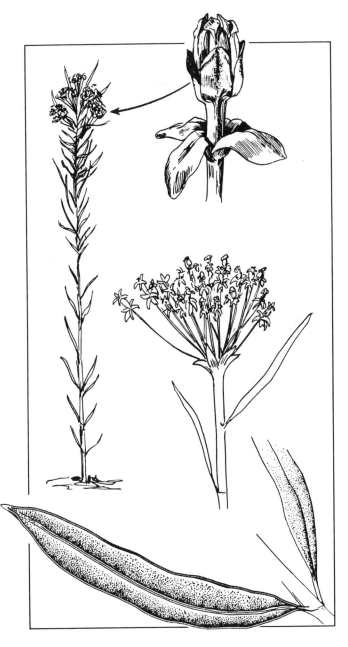

NAVAJO USES

MEDICINAL: *Ch'il'abe'éts'óóz* is one of the Navajo life medicines (see yarrow) that is used for stomach problems, skin diseases, and nose congestion. The medicine is prepared by crushing the leaves and mixing them with water. The liquid is taken internally. Crushed and moistened leaves are used as a poultice to treat pimples. Leaves are used as snuff to relieve nasal congestion. The milky looking sap helps nursing mothers produce milk.

CEREMONIAL: The silky hairs of *Ch'il'abe'éts'óóz* seeds are part of the ceremonial prayersticks.

OTHER: Poison milkweed is considered poisonous to all livestock. Luckily, animals seldom eat it if other food is available. Navajos say people can eat the plant, raw or boiled.

REFERENCES

Elmore, Francis, *Ethnobotany of the Navajo,* 69.

Matthews, Washington, "Navajo Names for Plants," *The American Naturalist,* 774.

Vestal, Paul A., *Ethnobotany of the Ramah Navajo,* 39.

Wyman, Leland, and Stuart Harris, *Navajo Indian Medical Ethnobotany,* 18, 23, 30–31, 44, 64.

Young Stella, *Native Plants Used by the Navajo,* 81, 95.

MISTLETOE *(Phoradendron)*
juniper mistletoe

Phoradendron juniperinum Engelm. (foo-ra-'den-dron jew-'nip-er-in-nuhm)
Phoradendron: The Greek words *phor,* "thief," and *dendron,* "tree," explain this plant's parasitic nature
juniperinum: Of the juniper

NAVAJO NAME: *Dahts'aa',* "basket on high"

DESCRIPTION & DISTRIBUTION

Juniper mistletoe is a drab, olive, many-stemmed, herbaceous, perennial plant with small, scalelike leaves. Stems are relatively stout and as long as 10 inches. Flowers are inconspicuous; fruits are yellowish to purplish.

This mistletoe is parasitic upon Utah juniper *(Juniperus osteosperma)* and oneseed juniper *(Juniperus monosperma)* almost wherever the two trees occur on the reservation, especially below 6,500 feet elevation.

NAVAJO USES

MEDICINAL: Juniper mistletoe is boiled with equal amounts of oneseed juniper *(Juniperus monosperma),* Rocky Mountain juniper *(Juniperus scopulorum),* and Colorado pinyon *(Pinus edulis)* to make a soothing lotion for ant or insect bites. The mistletoe juniper is also used to cure warts and to relieve stomach pains of hunters who eat too much fresh meat.

CEREMONIAL: *Dahts'aa'* is one of the plants used in Enemy Way medicine.

OTHER: The whole plant is edible. The berries can be eaten fresh and the stems boiled into a tea. However, neither tastes good, so today, the plant is not considered a food source.

Dahts'aa' branches collected from each of the four directions were hung in the doorway to protect the hogan from lightning.

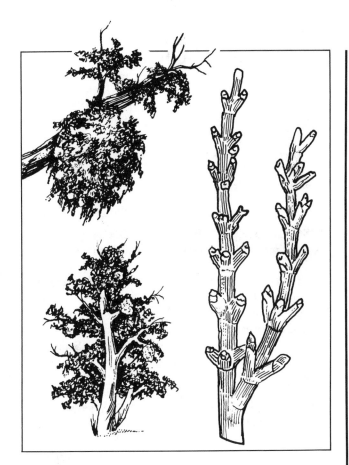

REFERENCES

Elmore, Francis, *Ethnobotany of the Navajo*, 41–42.

Hocking, George M., "Some Plant Materials Used Medicinally and Otherwise by the Navaho Indians in the Chaco Canyon, New Mexico," *El Palacio*, 162.

Matthews, Washington, "Navajo Names for Plants," *The American Naturalist*, 776.

Vestal, Paul A., *Ethnobotany of the Ramah Navajo*, 23.

Wyman, Leland, and Stuart Harris, *Navajo Indian Medical Ethnobotany*, 26, 38, 65.

Young, Stella, *Native Plants Used by the Navajo*, 5, 14.

MOCK-ORANGE *(Philadelphus)*
littleleaf mock-orange, syringa

Philadelphus microphyllus Gray. (fih-luh-'dell-fuss mih-cro-'fyel-luss)

Philadelphus: Named for Ptolemy Philadelphus II (309–246 B.C.), an Egyptian King who landscaped cities in his kingdom and founded a great Alexandrian library

microphyllus: From the Greek *micro,* "small," and *phyllon,* "leaf"

NAVAJO NAME: *Tsétsoh k'ịį'* "big rock sumac"

DESCRIPTION & DISTRIBUTION

Littleleaf mock-orange is a semierect, straggling, branchy shrub up to 4 feet tall. Young stems are tan to red-brown, becoming gray in age; older bark peels off in strips. Flowers resemble orange blossoms, white and showy. A family relative, cliff fendlerbush *(Fendlera rupicola)* is similar in appearance, but it has fewer stamens and tapering petal bases. Flowers late May through July.

From about 6,000 feet up to 8,000 feet in rock canyons on talus (rock slides) ledges and cliffs, littleleaf mock-orange is associated with cliff fendlerbush, common cliffrose *(Cowania mexicana),* mountain mahoganies *(Cercocarpus* sp.), sagebrushes *(Artemisia* sp.) and snowberries *(Symphoricarpos* sp.). At higher elevations to about 9,800 feet, it may associate more with rock spiraea *(Spiraea caespitosa),* mountain ninebark *(Physocarpus monogynus),* and Gambel oak *(Quercus gambelii).*

NAVAJO USES

CEREMONIAL: Littleleaf mock-orange is used in the preparations for the Navajo Striped Wind Way.

HOUSEHOLD: The wood of *tsétsoh k'ịį'* is burned for cooking and heating, and is used to make household items.

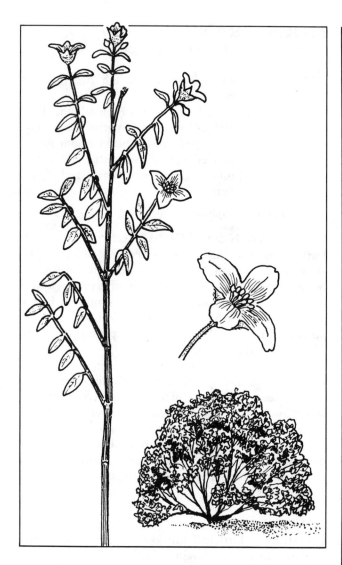

MOUNTAIN MAHOGANY *(Cercocarpus)*
alderleaf mountain mahogany, birchleaf mountain mahogany, featherbrush, palo duro

Cercocarpus montanus Raf. (ser-koh-'karp-us mon-'tay-nuss)
Cercocarpus: Greek for "shuttle-fruit," referring to the long tail
montanus: Of the mountains

NAVAJO NAME: *Tsé'ésdaazii,* "heavy as stone"

DESCRIPTION & DISTRIBUTION
Alderleaf mountain mahogany is a shrub sometimes attaining 7 feet in height. Stems are reddish brown, then pale gray, then darker as they age. Leaves somewhat resemble those of birch (*Betula* sp.), alder (*Alnus* sp.), and serviceberry (*Amelanchier* sp.), but are thick, coarsely but not doubly toothed down each side (to or past the middle), fuzzy, and clustered. Whitish flowers bloom May through September. The flowers have long curling, feathery "tails" as they wither.

Shrub communities of stony or rocky hillsides, ledges, and canyon rims are the neighborhoods for alderleaf mountain mahogany between elevations of 4,000 and 8,000 feet, but mostly between 6,000 and 8,000 feet. Close associates are curlleaf mountain mahogany *(Cercocarpus ledifolius),* common cliffrose *(Cowania mexicana),* Utah serviceberry *(Amelanchier utahensis),* cliff fendlerbush *(Fendlera rupicola),* and snowberries *(Symphoricarpos* sp.).

NAVAJO USES
MEDICINAL: The root and leaves of alderleaf mountain mahogany have an emetic action and are used to treat stomach problems. *Tsé'ésdaazii* is also given to a new mother to speed her recovery. The root is one of the Navajo life medicines (see yarrow).

CEREMONIAL: *Tsé'ésdaazii* is one of the plants used as an emetic in five- and nine-night ceremonies. It is used to

REFERENCES
Elmore, Francis, *Ethnobotany of the Navajo,* 52.
Wyman, Leland, and Stuart Harris, *Navajo Indian Medical Ethnobotany,* 21, 40.

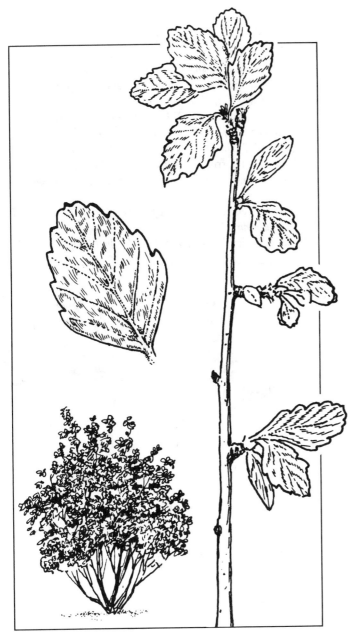

make ceremonial equipment or medicine in the Mountain Chant, Plume Way, and Chiricahua Wind Way.

OTHER: Alderleaf mountain mahogany is in demand for household items. Its hard wood is ideal for tool handles, weaving forks, and battens.

It is an excellent forage plant for sheep and deer. In fact, because deer like it so well, hunters chew the leaves from shrubs browsed by deer for good luck in hunting.

Alderleaf mountain mahogany was an early dye plant. A recipe written down in 1934 *(Navajo Weaving,* Charles Avery Amsden) says a red dye is produced by combining thinleaf alder *(Alnus incana),* birchleaf mountain mahogany, juniper *(Juniperus* sp.), and a lichen *(Parmelia* sp.). Other dyes using alderleaf mountain mahogany were developed by a home economics class at Fort Wingate High School, Fort Wingate, New Mexico, in the 1950s. *See appendix, page 141, for recipe.*

Alderleaf mountain mahogany is also used for basketry and leather dyes.

REFERENCES

Elmore, Francis, *Ethnobotany of the Navajo,* 39, 53.

Franciscan Fathers, *An Ethnologic Dictionary of the Navajo Language,* 198, 232—33, 242–43, 293, 304, 396, 407.

Hocking, George M., "Some Plant Materials Used Medicinally and Otherwise by the Navaho Indians in the Chaco Canyon, New Mexico," *El Palacio,* 159.

Kluckhohn, Clyde, et al., *Navajo Material Culture,* 342—43, 345-47.

Matthews, Washington, "Navajo Names for Plants," *The American Naturalist,* 772.

Vestal, Paul A., *Ethnobotany of the Ramah Navajo,* 30.

Wyman, Leland, and Stuart Harris, *Navajo Indian Medical Ethnobotany,* 22-23, 40, 57-58.

Young, Stella, *Native Plants Used by the Navajo,* 37, 49, 56-57, 64-67, 73.

NIGHTSHADE *(Solanum)*

*silverleaf nightshade, trompillo, white
horse-nettle*

Solanum elaeagnifolium Cav. (sol-'lay-num
el-ee-ag-nif-'foh-lee-um)
Solanum: From the Latin *solamen,* "solace" or "quieting."
A name probably given to this genus because
of the action of its strong chemical
components.
elaeagnifolium: Leaves like the olive tree; *elaeagnus,* is
Greek for the "olive and chaste tree" *(Vi-
tex agnus-castus); folium,* Latin for "leaf"

NAVAJO NAME: *Nááłtsoí,* "yellow eyes"

DESCRIPTION & DISTRIBUTION

Silverleaf nightshade is a perennial herb with an erect, simple, or branched stem up to 2 feet tall growing from
rhizomes (underground stems). Foliage and stems are
covered with grayish asterisklike hairs and usually with
yellowish prickles. Fruits are yellow to orange true berries. Gray-blue flowers bloom May through September.

Below elevations of about 6,500 feet, silverleaf
nightshade grows on coarse and medium soils along roadsides, trailsides, cultivated field margins, edges of washes,
and rims of swales.

NAVAJO USES

MEDICINAL: *Nááłtsoí* is used as a remedy for sore eyes, and
when dried and pulverized, as a remedy for nose and throat
trouble.

REFERENCES

Elmore, Francis, *Ethnobotany of the Navajo,* 37, 75.
Franciscan Fathers, *An Ethnologic Dictionary of the Navajo
Language,* 122, 200.
Steggerda, Morris, and T. M. Carpenter, "The Food of the
Present Day Navajo Indians of New Mexico and
Arizona," *The Journal of Nutrition,* 297–305.
Steggerda, Morris, and R. B. Eckardt, "Navajo Foods and
Their Preparation," *American Dietetic Association Journal,*
222.
Wyman, Leland, and Stuart Harris, *Navajo Indian Medical
Ethnobotany,* 17, 45, 70.
Young, Stella, *Native Plants Used by the Navajo,* 19.

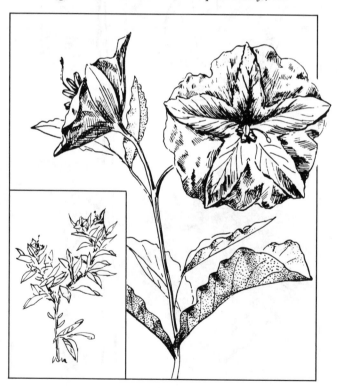

buffalobur

Solanum rostratum Dunal (sol-'lay-num ross-'tray-tum)
rostratum: Beaked or hooked

NAVAJO NAME: *Mą'ii ná'ooljił ch'il,* "Coyote against-lust-plant"

DESCRIPTION & DISTRIBUTION

Buffalobur is a short, branched, semierect, prickly, annual herb seldom taller than about 1 foot. Stems are yellow. Potatolike leaves are dull green above, very fuzzy below and about 8½ inches long. Flowers are yellow, produce prickly burs, and appear from early July through early September.

Stands of buffalobur are scattered across the reservation, below about 6,800 feet, in depressions and rills, along shores and dirt roadsides, and around fields where there is disturbance and extra soil moisture. Among its associates are white horse-nettle *(Solanum elaeagnifolium),* Texas dove-weed *(Croton texensis),* and pigweeds *(Amaranthus* sp.).

NAVAJO USES

CEREMONIAL: *Mą'ii ná'ooljił ch'il* was used in the Whirling Coyote ceremony.

OTHER: The yellow berries are used to make a goat's milk cottage cheese. Two berries are crushed and added to one quart of goat's milk. The mixture is boiled 5 minutes, drained, and eaten immediately.

REFERENCES

Personal communications, February 1980.
Wyman, Leland, and Stuart Harris, *Navajo Indian Medical Ethnobotany,* 30, 45.

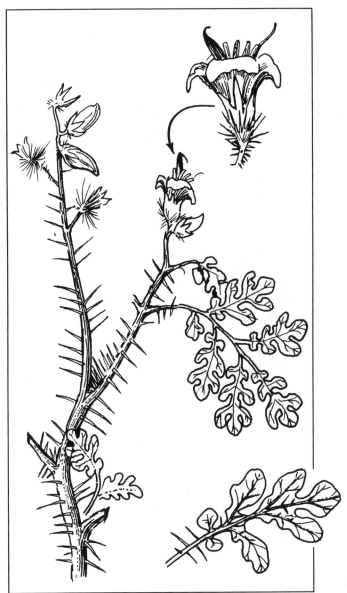

OAK *(Quercus)*
Gambel oak, Rocky Mountain white oak

Quercus gambelii Nutt. ('kwurk-us 'gam-bull-eye)
Quercus: Classic name for the oak tree, which was sacred
 to Jupiter, a Greek god.
gambelii: Named for Dr. William Gambel (1819–49),
 a Philadelphia ornithologist and botanist,
 who collected birds and plants in the West in
 the 1840s. The Gambel quail and three other
 birds were also named for him.

NAVAJO NAME: *Tsé'ch'il,* "rock plant"

DESCRIPTION & DISTRIBUTION
Gambel oak is the most common of the three oaks of
Navajoland and is quite different from the other two. It may
be a shrub or a tree as tall as 30 feet but is usually much
shorter. Young stems are brownish but turn gray with age;
old bark is dark gray and rough. Leaves are deciduous,
green, deeply lobed, and about 2 to 4 inches long on
yellow-green leaf stems. The acorns are much broader than
are those of shrub live oak *(Quercus turbinella)* or wavyleaf
oak *(Quercus undulata).*

Growing best—attaining tree size—at about 7,800 feet,
Gambel oak ranges down to about 4,500 feet in canyons
and up to about 9,800 feet on south slopes of mountains.
As a shrub, often in thickets, it is conspicuous in
communities of gooseberries *(Ribes* sp.), Arizona rose *(Rosa
arizonica),* cliff fendlerbush *(Fendlera rupicola),* and Utah
serviceberry *(Amelanchier utahensis);* and of mountain
mahoganies *(Cercocarpus* sp.), roundleaf buffaloberry
(Shepherdia rotundifolia), snowberries *(Symphoricarpos* sp.),
and rock spiraea *(Spiraea caespitosa).* As a tree, it forms a
forest with ponderosa pine *(Pinus ponderosa)* and Douglas

fir *(Pseudotsuga menziesii).* Throughout its great altitudinal
range, its most frequent associate may be Utah serviceberry.

NAVAJO USES
HOUSEHOLD: The bow and the arrow used in hunting and
war were often made of oak. The Navajos say that the bow,
like most other items necessary to their early life, comes
from the Holy People. The bow was first mentioned in
print, though not described, by Father Alonso de
Benavides, in 1630. *See appendix, page 141, for a description
of the Navajo bow.*

Other items made of the hard oak wood included axe
handles, digging sticks, weaving tools, gathering baskets,
cactus pickers, the bow of the cradleboard, stirrups,
snowshoes, and hunting equipment such as throwing sticks
used to bring down an animal by breaking its legs.

Whole oak trees were used to cover summer shade
houses.

Gambel oak acorns can be eaten raw, roasted in ashes,
boiled, or dried and ground into a meal like cornmeal.
Nevertheless, they were not frequently eaten by the Navajo.

A tan wool dye was made from oak bark boiled with
raw alum (mineral substance found at the base of rock cliffs
on the reservation) as a mordant.

CEREMONIAL: *Tsé'ch'il* is used for the ceremonial hoop,
for a ceremonial emetic, and for the blackening in the Evil
Way ceremony.

A lightning-struck oak was used for ceremonial fire
drill tips, the medicine stoppers, and the bull-roarer in other
ceremonies.

MEDICINAL: Gambel oak rootbark is used in life
medicine (see yarrow) to help lessen afterbirth pains and
as a cathartic.

REFERENCES

Elmore, Francis, *Ethnobotany of the Navajo,* 41.

Franciscan Fathers, *An Ethnologic Dictionary of the Navajo Language,* 299, 318, 324.

Kluckhohn, Clyde, et al., *Navajo Material Culture,* 23–31, 33, 56–70, 198–200, 217, 292–94, 361–67, 381–84, 416.

Martin, Neils, *Common Range Plants,* 2.

Vestal, Paul A., *Ethnobotany of the Ramah Navajo,* 22.

Young, Stella, *Native Plants Used by the Navajo,* 14–16, 50, 73.

OLEASTER *(Elaeagnus)*
common Russian olive

Elaeagnus angustifolia L. (eh-lee-'ag-nuss
    an-gus-ti-'foh-lih-uh)
Elaeagnus: From the Greek *elaia,* "olive," and the Latin
                  agnus, "lamb," "pure," or "innocent"
angustifolia: From the Latin for narrow leaves: *angust,*
          "narrow," and *folia,* "leaves"

NAVAJO NAME: *Didzé łibáhii,* "gray fruit"

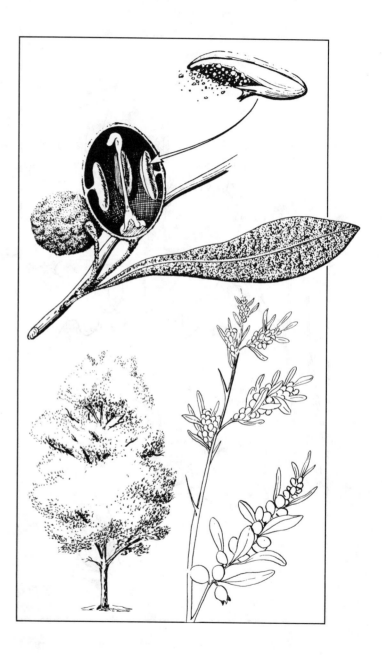

DESCRIPTION & DISTRIBUTION
Common Russian olive is often a tree in the wild, but seldom taller than about 15 feet. Foliage is deciduous and gray-green. Stems are dark brown. The tiny flowers are yellow. Fruits are about ⅜ inch long and darken with age. Flowers mostly in May.

    Along washes, streams, and lake shores between elevations of 4,500 and 7,000 feet, common Russian olive has displaced many willows (*Salix* sp.) in riparian groves. Its most frequent associate may be tamarisk (*Tamarix* sp.).

NAVAJO USES
Common Russian olive was introduced by the Spanish in the 1500s and has no historical Navajo use.

REFERENCES
    No written reference.

74

OPUNTIA *(Opuntia)*
Whipple cholla, tall prickly-pear

Opuntia whipplei Engelm & Bigel. (oh-'pun-shuh-uh
  'whip-pleye)
Opuntia: A misnamed genus. Theophrastus, of ancient
      Greece, gave the name to a different plant,
      which grew near the town of Opus.
whipplei: Named for Lt. A. W. Whipple, commander
      of the Pacific Railroad Expedition, 1853–54.

NAVAJO NAME: *Hosh dítsahiitsoh*, "big needle cactus"

DESCRIPTION & DISTRIBUTION
Whipple cholla is a sprawling shrub (cactus) seldom
exceeding 2 feet in height. It is the only cholla (cactus with
cylindrical stems) growing on the reservation proper
(excluding the New Mexico area.) Stems are yellowish
green and have tubercles (orderly bumps) on which are
short yellow glochids (hairlike spines) in a cluster around
the 4 to 6 principal spines (the central one may reach out
about ¾ inch). Flower petals and sepals are yellowish when
fresh. The fruits are bumpy and yellowish. Flowers June
through early August.

Below about 7,000 feet, in woodlands of Colorado
pinyon *(Pinus edulis)* and Utah juniper *(Juniperus
osteosperma);* in shrublands of big sagebrush *(Artemisia
tridentata)* and fourwing saltbush *(Atriplex canescens);* and in
shrublands of spiny saltbush *(Atriplex confertifolia)*,
blackbush *(Coleogyne ramosissima)*, and Torrey joint-fir
(Ephedra torreyana); Whipple cholla is sparsely distributed
on dry flats and uplands, usually on soils of coarse or
medium texture.

NAVAJO USES
CEREMONIAL: *Hosh dítsahiitsoh* is used to make cactus
prayersticks in the Apache Wind Way, and the wand in the
Red Ant Way. The wand is made with rabbitbrush
(Chrysothamnus nauseosus) and other plants wrapped with
yucca *(Yucca* sp.) fibers and five small wooden disks, each
painted a different color: white, yellow, blue, black, and
silver.

HOUSEHOLD: Navajos do not eat the fruit of Whipple
cholla. They say it is inedible, even poisonous.

REFERENCES
Vestal, Paul A., *Ethnobotany of the Ramah Navajo*, 37.

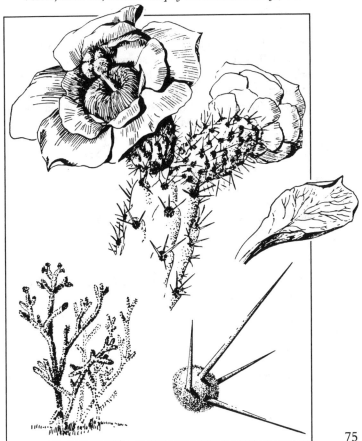

plains prickly-pear, many-spined cactus, cactus prickly-pear

Opuntia phaeacantha Engelm. (oh-'pun-shuh-uh
   fa-uh-'can-thuh)
phaeacantha: From the Greek *phaea,* "dark," and *akantha,*
   "thorn"

NAVAJO NAME: *Hosh niteelí,* "broad cactus"

DESCRIPTION & DISTRIBUTION
Plains prickly-pear is a short cactus forming small, waxy, greenish clumps of flattened, jointed, roundish stems under 1 foot tall. The pads (terminal stem sections) bear several principal spines and many glochids (short, stiff, sharp hairs) on most of the tubercles (orderly bumps) on the faces and margins (spines on bumps along the margins may be as long as 1¾ inches). Marginal bumps bear the yellow flowers and fruits. Flowers mostly in June.

Clumps of plains prickly-pear are scattered in woodlands of pinyon (*Pinus* sp.) and juniper (*Juniperus* sp.) and in overlapping woodland and forest between elevations of 6,000 and 7,200 feet (the higher elevations on south slopes). Broadleaf yucca *(Yucca baccata)* seems to be a common associate.

NAVAJO USES
MEDICINAL: The fleshy leaf is peeled and bound over a cut to stop the bleeding.

CEREMONIAL: Cactus People are part of the Navajo origin myth, and thus, cactus is used in several ceremonies.

OTHER: The sweet juicy fruit of the plains prickly-pear was eaten by the Navajos, fresh, dried, or cooked in a stew with dried peaches. *See appendix, page 142, for nutritional composition.* The spines of the fruit were removed by rolling the fruit in sand or by singeing it in hot ashes.

The sticky juice from cactus stems was used as glue in making the buckskin war shield.

76

The cactus was used to make an arrow poison. A mixture of rattlesnake blood, yucca (*Yucca* sp.) juice, and charcoal from the pith of the cactus was painted on at least six inches of an arrow.

A variety of rose and pink dyes can be made from the ripe cactus fruit. The riper or darker the fruit, the darker the dye. A rose dye is made by steeping ripe prickly-pear fruit and bark or roots of Colorado blue spruce (*Picea pungens*) in water.

REFERENCES

Elmore, Francis, *Ethnobotany of the Navajo,* 65.

Matthews, Washington, "Navajo Names for Plants," *The American Naturalist,* 773.

Wyman, Leland, and Stuart Harris, *Navajo Indian Medical Ethnobotany,* 27.

Young, Stella, *Native Plants Used by the Navajo,* 12, 60–61.

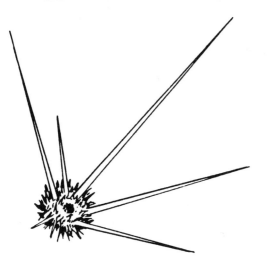

PIGWEED *(Amaranthus)*
prostrate pigweed

Amaranthus graecizans L. (am-ar-'anth-us 'greek-uh-zans)
Amaranthus: From the Greek *amarantos,* "unfading." The new Latin *amaranthus* incorporates the Latin word for flower, *anthus.* Thus the word now means unfading flower.
graecizans: Now means "becoming widespread"; may be in reference to the spread of the Greek language and culture over all of the known world in the time of Alexander the Great.

NAVAJO NAME: *Naazkaadii,* "spread out"

DESCRIPTION & DISTRIBUTION

Prostrate pigweed is a dull green annual herb with many prostrate stems radiating from the root crown. As the season progresses, stems may change from green to yellow to purple. Flowers are the same color as the foliage and lack petals. Stems may grow to about 2 feet; leaves seldom exceed 1 inch. Flowers late July through September.

Gardens, fields, and other disturbed sites with extra soil moisture and medium to fine soils (below about 8,000 feet) are often occupied by a community of puncture vine (*Tribulus terrestris*), field bindweed (*Convolvulus arvensis*), prostrate pigweed, common knotweed (*Polygonum aviculare*), and Russian thistle (*Salsola iberica*).

NAVAJO USES

CEREMONIAL: *Naazkaadii* is part of the tobacco in the Coyote Chant.

HOUSEHOLD: The seeds of prostrate pigweed were once a food source for the Navajos. They were threshed and ground into a flour or made into a mush with goat's milk. Sheep eat this pigweed.

REFERENCES

Elmore, Francis, *Ethnobotany of the Navajo*, 45.

Franciscan Fathers, *An Ethnologic Dictionary of the Navajo Language*, 181.

Matthews, Washington, "Navajo Names for Plants," *The American Naturalist*, 775.

Vestal, Paul A., *Ethnobotany of the Ramah Navajo*, 25–26.

Wyman, Leland, and Stuart Harris, *Navajo Indian Medical Ethnobotany*, 31.

Young, Stella, *Native Plants Used by the Navajo*, 7, 30, 32, 80.

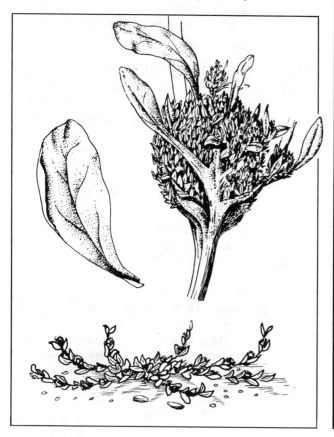

PINE *(Pinus)*
pinyon, Colorado pinyon, twoleaf pinyon, nut pine

Pinus edulis Engelm. ('pye–nus ed–'yew-liss)
Pinus: Pine, the name from Roman times
edulis: Edible

NAVAJO NAMES: *Chá'oł*, "pinyon" (*Neeshch'íí*, "pinyon seeds"; *Atlish*, "pinyon butter"; *Deestsiin*, "pinyon logs"; *Deestsiin bijeeh*, "pinyon gum")

DESCRIPTION & DISTRIBUTION

Colorado pinyon is the only one of the three southwestern pinyons on the reservation. It is a tree of small to medium size (up to about 30 feet) with a rounded, fairly dense crown, red-brown bark, and squat cones only sporadically produced in large numbers. Needles are ¾ to 1½ inches long and are usually in bundles of 2; other pinyons bear needles singly or in groups of 3.

Within its range, from 4,000 to 9,000 feet, Colorado pinyon is most abundant, tallest, and dominant in the woodland of Colorado pinyon, Utah juniper (*Juniperus osteosperma*), and big sagebrush (*Artemisia tridentata*) on soils of various textures. It is also significant in communities of ponderosa pine *(Pinus ponderosa)*, Colorado pinyon, Gambel oak *(Quercus gambelii)*, and Rocky Mountain juniper *(Juniperus scopulorum)*; and of Utah juniper *(Juniperus osteosperma)*, oneseed juniper *(Juniperus monosperma)*, and Colorado pinyon.

NAVAJO USES

MEDICINAL: Pinyon pitch is mixed with red clay and mutton tallow to make a skin salve much like Vaseline. The recipe is a spoonful of red clay mixed with ¾ cup of melted mutton tallow. Melted pinyon pitch is worked into this mixture and the salve is used warm to sooth skin irritations or to protect skin from sunburn.

Rotted pine wood can be ground into a talcum powder for babies.

Pinyon pitch is used as an emetic; the leaves are boiled with juniper leaves to treat diarrhea.

CEREMONIAL: Pinyon is used for medicine or equipment in almost every Navajo ceremony. It is used to build ceremonial hogans and corrals for the Mountain Chant and Night Chant. Pinyon charcoal is preferred for the black pigment in sandpainting.

Pinyon pitch is used in the ritual necessary after the death of a relative or friend.

OTHER: Pinyon seeds are a favorite and nutritious snack on the Navajo Reservation. They are an excellent source of protein, niacin, riboflavin, and calories. Seeds may be eaten raw, roasted in a skillet, or mashed into a seed butter, called *atlish*, after roasting. *See appendix, page 142, for nutritional content.*

Pinyon seeds have always been a valuable trade item. A million pounds of pinyon seeds from the Navajo Reservation were shipped east in 1936.

Pinyon gum is chewed for its flavor.

The sticky pitch gives Navajo wickerwork its unusual glasslike coating and Navajo pottery its tantalizing shine. Navajo pitched-baskets, *tóshjeeh*, are usually woven of sumac (*Rhus* sp.) or willow (*Salix* sp.) with a ball-shaped body and a high, narrow neck. If they are somewhat crudly woven it doesn't matter because they are coated inside and out with pinyon pitch. Pitch is heated, then poured into the basket as it is rotated so the pitch covers the inside completely.

Pitch for the exterior of the basket is mixed with a small amount of red clay to give the basket a reddish brown color. A heated pebble is used to smooth the coating.

Navajo pottery, *łeets'aa'*, is made with local clays tempered with pottery sherds. Favorite shapes are tall vaselike cooking vessels and gourd-shaped ladles. Potters use a coil method and smooth the clay with water and a

79

corncob, piece of gourd, or smooth stone.

The pottery is buried in sheep manure and covered with hot ashes for firing. Pinyon-gum coating is painted on after firing.

At one time pinyon pitch was used to cement turquoise stones into silverwork.

Pinyon pitch is used to make a black dye.

REFERENCES

Bailey, Flora, "Navajo Foods and Cooking Methods," *American Anthropologist,* 287.

Elmore, Francis, *Ethnobotany of the Navajo,* 21–23.

Franciscan Fathers, *An Ethnologic Dictionary of the Navajo Language,* 47, 230, 243, 256, 267, 288, 293, 297–98, 303–304, 318, 334–35, 400, 409, 415, 458–59.

Hocking, George M., "Some Plant Materials Used Medicinally and Otherwise by the Navaho Indians in the Chaco Canyon, New Mexico," *El Palacio,* 162.

Kluckhohn, Clyde, et al., *Navajo Material Culture,* 140–41.

Steggerda, Morris, and R. B. Eckardt, "Navajo Foods and Their Preparation," *American Dietetic Association Journal,* 222.

Tschopik, Harry Jr., *Navajo Pottery Making,* 14, 20, 40–41.

Watt, B. K., and A. L. Merrill, et al., *Composition of Foods, Agricultural Handbook No. 8,* 46.

Wyman, Leland, and Stuart Harris, *Navajo Indian Medical Ethnobotany,* 23, 36, 58.

Young, Stella, *Native Plants Used by the Navajo,* 16–18, 34, 42–45, 110.

ponderosa pine, western yellow pine

Pinus ponderosa Lawson ('pye-nus pon-der-'roh-suh)
ponderosa: Heavy, massive

NAVAJO NAME: *Nídíshchíí,* "the pine"

DESCRIPTION & DISTRIBUTION

Ponderosa pine, one of the yellow pines (the only one in Navajoland), is the largest pine and second largest conifer on the reservation. Attaining a height of about 100 feet and a diameter of about 3 feet, it towers over all other trees except Douglas fir. Twigs are yellowish with 5-inch-long needles in bundles of 3 and 2. Bark changes from dark gray-brown to brownish to yellowish brown as it ages. Seedbearing cones are brown and about 4 inches long. The seed scales have prickles.

Within its range from the Engelmann spruce *(Picea engelmannii)* and quaking aspen *(Populus tremuloides)* community at 9,500 feet, down to riparian (streamside) communities in canyons at 6,000 feet, ponderosa pine dominates the forest between 7,000 and 8,000 feet. Among its conspicuous associates are Colorado pinyon *(Pinus edulis),* Gambel oak *(Quercus gambelii),* Rocky Mountain juniper *(Juniperus scopulorum),* Colorado blue spruce *(Picea pungens),* and Douglas fir *(Pseudotsuga menziesii).*

NAVAJO USES

MEDICINAL: Yellow pine is a cold and fever medicine.

CEREMONIAL: *Nídíshchíí'* is used for medicine and equipment in at least six ceremonies: Chiricahua Wind Way, Enemy Way, Evil Way, Night Chant, Red Ant Way, and Big Star Way. For example, pieces of ponderosa pine bark are used as trays for sandpainting pigments.

OTHER: This large tree is used where heavy construction materials are needed: hogans, corrals, sweathouses, and fences. It is also used for delicate items like the cradleboard,

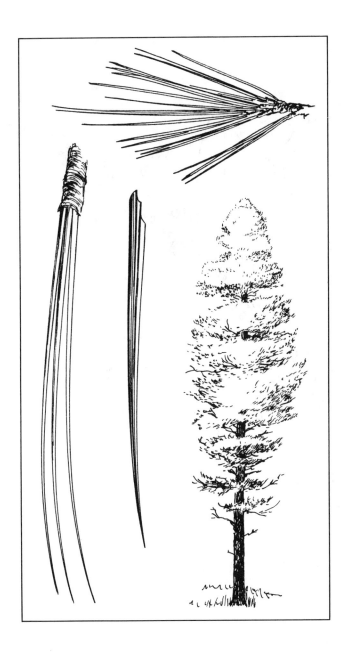

awééts'ááł. See appendix, page 143, for further discussion on cradleboards.

The inner bark is edible, the outer bark produces a red dye, and the burls were once used for ladles or large spoons.

REFERENCES

Elmore, Francis, *Ethnobotany of the Navajo*, 23.

Franciscan Fathers, *An Ethnologic Dictionary of the Navajo Language*, 31, 66–67.

Kluckhohn, Clyde, et al., *Navajo Material Culture*, 144, 191, 416–19.

Locke, Raymond, *The Book of the Navajo*, 24.

Wyman, Leland, and Stuart Harris, *Ethnobotany of the Kayenta Navajo*, 15, 61.

———, *Navajo Indian Medical Ethnobotany*, 31, 36, 73–74.

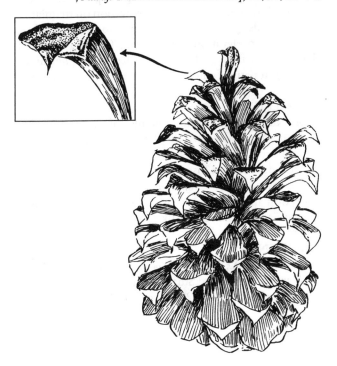

PLANTAIN *(Plantago)*
common plantain

Plantago major L. (plan-'tay-goh 'may-jor)
Plantago: From the Latin *planta*, meaning the "sole of the
       foot"; in reference to this genus' wide leaves
major: From the Latin *major*, "greater"

NAVAJO NAME: *Biih yiljaa'í*, "like a deer's ear"

DESCRIPTION & DISTRIBUTION
Common plantain is a small, perennial herb with broad
leaves growing directly from the caudex (root crown) and
with a leafless, flowering stalk up to almost 1 foot tall. Leaf
blades are 2½ by 4 inches to 3 by 6 inches. Flowers are small
and whitish and appear May through September.

Distributed throughout the reservation on frequently
watered soils (lawns, fields, basins, flooding benches,
shores) up to elevations of about 7,700 feet, common
plantain associates with common dandelion *(Taraxacum
officinale)* in natural communities of riparian vegetation.

NAVAJO USES
MEDICINAL: The root of common plantain is one of the life
medicines (see yarrow). The plant is used to treat many
internal problems: indigestion, stomachache, heartburn,
venereal disease, and loss of appetite. It is also a diuretic.

CEREMONIAL: *Biih yiljaa'í* is used in the prayers for
protection in the Deer Way and is also smoked for a
ceremonial tobacco. The stalk is a ceremonial lighter.

REFERENCES
Vestal, Paul A., *Ethnobotany of the Ramah Navajo*, 45.
Wyman, Leland, and Stuart Harris, *Navajo Indian Medical
    Ethnobotany*, 17–18, 21, 24, 46, 56, 60–61.

82

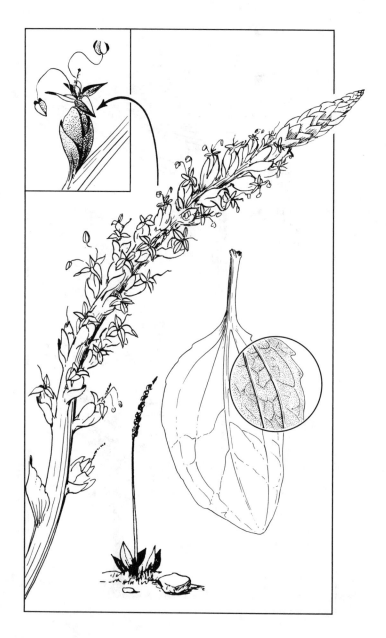

PRINCE'S PLUME *(Stanleya)*
prince's plume, desert plume

Stanleya pinnata (Pursh) Britt. ('stan-lee-uh
   pin-'nay-tuh)
Stanleya: Named after Sir Henry Morton (1841–1904),
        an English ornithologist, author, and plant
        explorer
pinnata: From the Latin, *pinna,* "feather," meaning in
        botany, having leaflets or divisions in a feather-
        like arrangement on either side of a common
        axis, as many compound leaves do

NAVAJO NAME: *Tséyaa hataał,* "sings under rock"

DESCRIPTION & DISTRIBUTION

Prince's plume is a perennial, herbaceous plant with a
woody root crown and stem base. Height is usually under
4½ feet. Stout stems arise from branches of the root crown;
they and their large leaves are neither hairy nor very waxy.
Yellow flowers bloom in late April through early October.

    This conspicuous plant occurs at 6,000 feet and below
in shrublands of spiny saltbush *(Atriplex confertifolia)* and
Torrey joint-fir *(Ephedra torreyana);* of fourwing saltbush
(Atriplex canescens) and black greasewood *(Sarcobatus
vermiculatus);* and of big sagebrush *(Artemisia tridentata),*
Greene rabbitbrush *(Chrysothamnus greenei),* and broom
snakeweed *(Gutierrezia sarothrae).* Often the sites are barren,
plants are scattered, and soil is medium to fine in texture.
Stanleya sp. is an obligate species of seleniferous soils. It
requires soils high in selenium for normal growth.

NAVAJO USES

MEDICINAL: Prince's plume is used as an emetic and as a
medicine for glandular swellings. It is also one of the life
medicines (see yarrow).
    CEREMONIAL: *Tséyaa hataał* is an Evil Way emetic.

83

OTHER: This showy desert plant is said to have been used as a food.

REFERENCES

Dodge, Natt, *100 Desert Wildflowers in Natural Color*, 23.
Elmore, Francis, *Ethnobotany of the Navajo*, 50.
Matthews, Washington, "Navajo Names for Plants," *The American Naturalist*, 770.
Wyman, Leland, and Stuart Harris, *Ethnobotany of the Kayenta Navajo*, 25.
————, *Navajo Indian Medical Ethnobotany*, 21–22, 40, 57,73.
Young, Stella, *Native Plants Used by the Navajo*, 96.

PUNCTURE VINE *(Tribulus)*
puncture vine, bur nut, caltrop

Tribulus terrestris L. (trib-'bul-lus ter-'res-triss)
Tribulus: Named after a Roman *tribulus,* a three-pronged iron implement used to impede the cavalry
terrestris: From the Latin, "growing on the soil," as opposed to growing on rocks or trees

NAVAJO NAME: *Béégashii bitsiits'iin,* "bull head"

DESCRIPTION & DISTRIBUTION
Puncture vine is a prostrate to semierect, vinelike (but not climbing), annual herb with stems spreading outward as far as 2 feet from the root crown. Foliage has silklike hairs. Fruits are burlike and armed with sharp projections. Flowers July through August.

Below 7,000 feet, puncture vine flourishes on disturbed and cultivated areas where there is extra water from irrigation, sporadic inundation, or impoundment. Its close associates are field bindweed *(Convolvulus arvensis),* prostrate pigweed *(Amaranthus graecizans),* and common knotweed *(Polygonum aviculare).*

NAVAJO USES
CEREMONIAL: *Béégashii bitsiits'iin* is one of the plants used as ceremonial tobacco in the Evil Way and Bead Way. The others are starflower *(Gilia longiflora),* spreading four o'clock *(Mirabilis oxybaphoides),* scurf pea *(Psoralea tenuiflora),* and catchfly *(Silene douglasii).* Puncture vine is a medicine in other ceremonies and a blackening in the Evil Way.

REFERENCES

Elmore, Francis, *Ethnobotany of the Navajo,* 59, 82.

Franciscan Fathers, *An Ethnologic Dictionary of the Navajo Language,* 201, 395.

Hocking, George M., "Some Plant Materials Used Medicinally and Otherwise by the Navaho Indians in the Chaco Canyon, New Mexico," *El Palacio,* 163.

Martin, Neils, *Common Range Plants,* 3.

Wyman, Leland, and Stuart Harris, *Navajo Indian Medical Ethnobotany,* 18, 42.

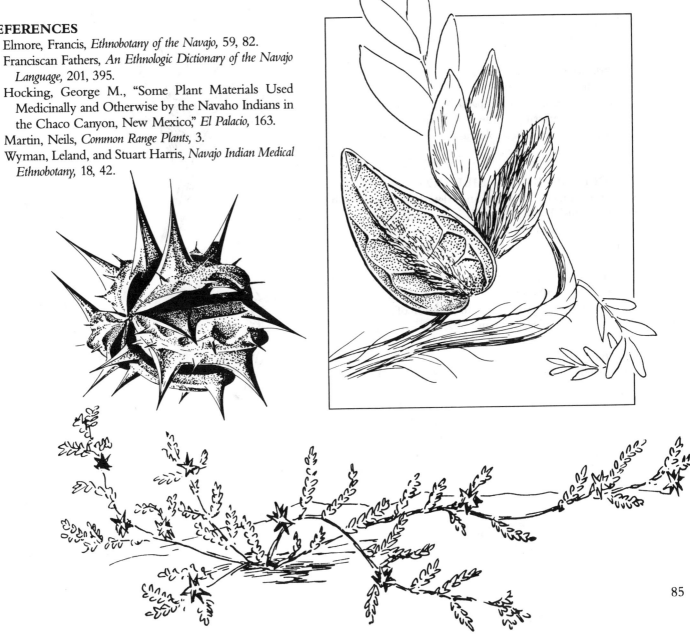

PURSLANE *(Portulaca)*
common purslane, pussley, verdolage

Portulaca oleracea L. (port-yew-'lay-kuh
   oh-ler-'ray-see-uh)
Portulaca: From the Latin *porta*, "carry," and *lac*, "milky,"
   referring to the milky juice
oleracea: Of the vegetable garden or kitchen

NAVAJO NAME: *Tségha'niłchi',* "breeze through rock"

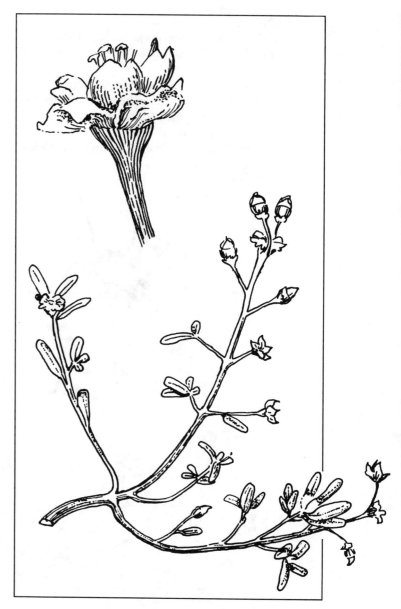

DESCRIPTION & DISTRIBUTION
Common purslane is a fleshy annual with matlike reddish
stems, greenish leaves, and small, inconspicuous yellowish
flowers. It resembles the so-called rubber plant grown
ornamentally in pots inside. Flowers July through
September.

   On soils of medium or fine texture, in swales where
water sporadically puddles, and as a weed in fields,
common purslane grows up to an elevation of about 7,000
feet. It is an invader of disturbed areas.

NAVAJO USES
MEDICINAL: The plant is said to cure stomachache and is
used in a smoke treatment to clean out the body; the smoke
causes the patient to vomit and thus, cleans him out.

   OTHER: Mush and bread can be made from the seeds.
The leaves are used as greens, either boiled alone or with
stews. *See appendix, page 143, for nutritional composition.*

   The plant is considered to have little food value for
animals.

REFERENCES

Elmore, Francis, *Ethnobotany of the Navajo,* 47.

Hocking, George M., "Some Plant Materials Used Medicinally and Otherwise by the Navaho Indians in the Chaco Canyon, New Mexico," *El Palacio,* 154.

Vestal, Paul A., *Ethnobotany of the Ramah Navajo,* 26.

Watt, B. K., and A. L. Merrill, et al., *Composition of Foods, Agricultural Handbook No. 8,* 51.

Wyman, Leland, and Stuart Harris, *Ethnobotany of the Kayenta Navajo,* 22, 61.

——— , *Navajo Indian Medical Ethnobotany,* 22, 39.

Young, Stella, *Native Plants Used by the Navajo,* 30.

RABBITBRUSH *(Chrysothamnus)*
rubber rabbitbrush, heavy-scented rabbitbrush, false-goldenrod

Chrysothamnus nauseosus (Pall.) Britt. (krih-soh-'tham-nuss naw-seh-'oh-sus)
Chrysothamnus: Greek for "golden bush"
nauseosus: From the Latin and Greek words for seasickness *nausia,* "producing sickness or nausea"; the Greek *naus* means "ship"

NAVAJO NAME: *K'iłtsoí nitsaaígíí,* "big yellow on top"

DESCRIPTION & DISTRIBUTION

Rubber rabbitbrush is a fairly densely branched, gray-green shrub growing up to about 5 feet in height. It is quite similar to sticky-flowered rabbitbrush *(Chrysothamnus viscidiflorus)* but is bigger and has a feltlike covering on the twigs. Superficially, it resembles the bigger of the goldenweeds *(Aplopappus* sp.). Loose clusters of heads of tiny yellow flowers bloom August through October.

Within its elevational range (about 3,800 to 8,000 feet), rubber rabbitbrush is of greatest stature and is most common in pinyon-juniper *(Pinus edulis* and *Juniperus* sp.) woodlands and sagebrush-saltbush *(Artemisia* sp. and *Atriplex* sp.) shrublands between 5,000 and 7,000 feet on soils of all textures.

NAVAJO USES

MEDICINAL: Rubber rabbitbrush is used for coughs, colds, fever, rheumatism, internal injuries, headache, and menstrual pain and as an emetic and cathartic.

CEREMONIAL: *K'iłtsoí nitsaaígíí* is used as medicine in at least five ceremonies: Beauty Way, Evil Way, Game Way, Holy Way, and both the male and female branches of the Shooting Way.

HOUSEHOLD: A part of the plant, possibly the seed, was once used as a leavener for cornbread or added to cornmeal mush as it cooked.

Rubber rabbitbrush's main use among the Navajo is as a dye: the top of the plant will produce a yellow wool and basket dye. A clear yellow comes from boiling only the mature yellow blossoms; a greenish tint comes from using the immature flowers, leaves, or green bark. *See appendix, page 144, for dye recipe.*

The greens can be added to wild onions *(Allium* sp.), wild celery *(Apiastrum* sp.), and meat stews, or can be fried, or dried and saved for winter.

The seeds can be made into mush or bread.

REFERENCES

Dodge, Natt, *100 Roadside Wildflowers of the Southwest Uplands,* 76.

Elmore, Francis, *Ethnobotany of the Navajo,* 83.

Hocking, George M., "Some Plant Materials Used Medicinally and Otherwise by the Navaho Indians in the Chaco Canyon, New Mexico," *El Palacio,* 159.

Vestal, Paul A., *Ethnobotany of the Ramah Navajo,* 49, 80.

Wyman, Leland, and Stuart Harris, *Ethnobotany of the Kayenta Navajo,* 46, 61.

Young, Stella, *Native Plants Used by the Navajo,* 51, 77.

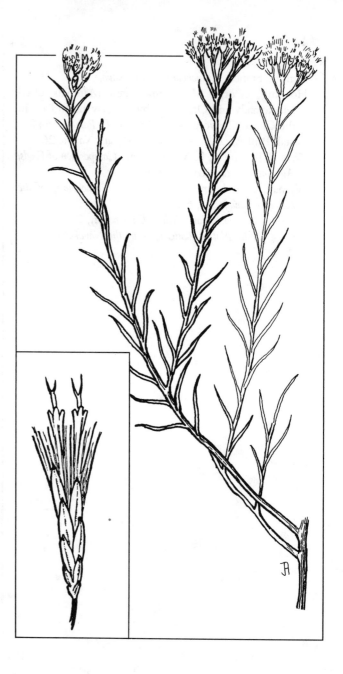

COLOR PLATES

Numbers in captions correspond to page on which discussion of plant begins.

Thinleaf alder, 4

Scarlet false-mallow, 5

Arrowgrass, 7

Manyflowered baby-aster, 8

Fremont barberry, 9

Creeping barberry, 10

Bearded penstemon, 11

Rocky Mountain beeplant, 12

Parry bellflower, 14

Field bindweed, 15

Water birch, 16

Colorado rubberweed, 17

Blackbrush, 18

Yellow mentzelia, 19

Mountain lover, 20

Bracken fern, 21

Cheatgrass brome, 22

Cutleaf coneflower, 23

Roundleaf buffaloberry, 24

Southern cattail, 25

Common chokecherry, 26

Common cliffrose, 27

Common cocklebur, 28

Fremont cottonwood, 29

Texas doveweed, 31

Golden crownbeard, 32

Curly-leaf dock, 33

Creeping dogwood, 35

White-stemmed evening primrose, 36

Subalpine fir, 37

Colorado four o'clock, 38

Galleta, 39

Few-leaved gilia, 40

Oyster plant, 41

Wild currant, 42

Common lambsquarters, 43

Blue grama, 45

Black greasewood, 46

Threadleaf groundsel, 48

Rayless gumweed, 49

93

Redstem filaree, 50

Common horehound, 51

Common horsetail, 52

Rocky Mountain iris, 53

Torrey joint-fir, 54

Utah juniper, 55

Rocky Mountain juniper, 57

Nelson larkspur, 58

Spotted loco, 59

Silvery lupine, 60

94

Roundleaf mallow, 61

Greenleaf manzanita, 62

Inland box elder, 63

Golden mariposa, 64

Whorled milkweed, 65

Juniper mistletoe, 66

Littleleaf mock-orange, 67

Alderleaf mountain mahogany, 68

Silverleaf nightshade, 70

95

Buffalobur, 71

Gambel oak, 72

Common Russian olive, 74

Whipple cholla, 75

Plains prickly-pear, 76

Prostrate pigweed, 77

Pinyon, 78

Ponderosa pine, 80

Common plantain, 82

96

Prince's plume, 83

Puncture vine, 84

Common purslane, 86

Rubber rabbitbrush, 87

Common reed, 101

Indian ricegrass, 102

Wire rush, 104

Tumbleweed, 105

Big sagebrush, 106

Spiny saltbush, 108

Fourwing saltbush, 109

Wooton sandpuff, 111

Golden smoke, 112

Utah serviceberry, 113

Broom snakeweed, 115

Narrowleaf yucca, 116

Common spectaclepod, 118

Prairie spiderwort, 119

Fendler spurge, 120

Skunkbush, 122

Annual sunflower, 124

Yellow sweet-clover, 125

French tamarisk, 127

Purple three-awn, 128

Hoary ground-daisy, 129

Spike verbena, 130

Virginia creeper, 131

99

Western wheatgrass, 132

Redroot wild buckwheat, 133

Coyote willow, 134

Desert wolfberry, 136

Western yarrow, 137

REED *(Phragmites)*
common reed

Phragmites australis (Cav.) Trin. ex Steud. (fray-'my-teez
'ost-ray-liss)
Phragmites: Phragma, is Greek for "fence" or screen"; a
reference to this plant's hedgelike growth
along ditches
australis: Southern

NAVAJO NAME: *Lók'aa*', "reed"

DESCRIPTION & DISTRIBUTION

Common reed is the largest native grass of Navajoland;
it may attain heights of about 8 feet. Stout, hollow stems
with large flat leaves and terminal tassellike flower clusters
arise from the long surface and subterranean runners.
Foliage of this coarse perennial is gray-green. Flowers are
open July through September, turning from whitish to
purplish in color.

Below about 6,200 feet, common reed grows on soils
of various textures around water impoundments and along
washes, streams, and irrigation ditches. Its associates are
usually inland saltgrass *(Distichlis stricta),* rushes (*Juncus* sp.),
sedges (*Carex* sp.), willows (*Salix* sp.), sunflowers
(*Helianthus* sp.), and beeplants (*Cleome* sp.).

NAVAJO USES

MEDICINAL: *Lók'aa'* is one of several emetic-acting plants
used for stomach and skin problems.

CEREMONIAL: In the Navajo emergence story, one of
the Holy People gave *lók'aa'* to the Navajos so they could
escape from the rapidly rising waters of the fourth world.
People, animals, and insects crowded into the magical reed,
which rapidly grew to the sky. To keep it from swaying
in the wind, one of the Holy People took a feather from

his headdress and stuck it through the top of the reed to secure it to the sky. Today, the featherlike, tassellike, flower cluster is a reminder to the Navajo of their escape from the flood into the fifth world.

The reed is used for ceremonial equipment, especially for prayersticks in all ceremonies.

OTHER: Although the common reed is said to have been used as an arrowshaft, Navajos say it is much too delicate for this.

REFERENCES

Elmore, Francis, *Ethnobotany of the Navajo,* 26.
Franciscan Fathers, *An Ethnologic Dictionary of the Navajo Language,* 31, 190, 318–19.
Kluckhohn, Clyde, et al., *Navajo Material Culture,* 36, 40, 347.
Locke, Raymond, F., *The Book of the Navajo,* 73.
Matthews, Washington, "Navajo Names for Plants," *The American Naturalist,* 777.
Wyman, Leland, and Stuart Harris, *Navajo Indian Medical Ethnobotany,* 29, 36, 57–58.

RICEGRASS *(Oryzopsis)*
Indian ricegrass, sand bunchgrass, mountain-rice, Indian millet, silk grass

Oryzopsis hymenoides (R. & S.) Ricker. (oryz-'op-sis hye-men-'noy-deez)
Oryzopsis: From the Greek *oryza,* "rice," and *opsis,* "appearance"
hymenoides: Membranelike

NAVAJO NAME: *Nididlídii,* "scorched"

DESCRIPTION & DISTRIBUTION
Indian ricegrass is a gray-green, tufted bunchgrass about 1¾ feet tall. Leaves are narrow, inrolled, and the blades are up to 1 foot long. Leaf sheaths enveloping stem bases change from yellowish to brownish as they age and may become mottled with black. Many small spikelets are clustered at the ends of stems; a spikelet contains the floret (reduced flower) and changes from gray-green to purplish with time. Flowers April through June.

Indian ricegrass is one of the few plants growing on sand dunes; it usually occupies coarse soils. It is the major grass in communities of saltbushes (*Atriplex* sp.), joint-firs (*Ephedra* sp.), and black greasewood *(Sarcobatus vermiculatus)* below about 5,500 feet. Within its elevational range of 3,800 to 7,000 feet, it is somewhat sparse in the woodlands and forests above 6,500 feet.

NAVAJO USES
HOUSEHOLD: Scorched grass was an early Navajo food. It is not used today, probably because it is so difficult to prepare.

The seeds are covered with a persistent chaff, which must be removed before the seeds can be eaten. Traditionally, the grass was picked in a bunch and held over the fire to burn off the chaff. As it burned, the seeds fell into a metate or skillet. The scorched seeds were ground

and cooked with milk or water to make mush, dumplings, or cakes, which were baked in ashes.

Sometimes the whole plant was burnt to ashes, ground, and the powder added to goat's milk or made into bread.

Nididlídii is a good food for horses, cattle, goats, and wild animals.

Early Navajo clothing and bedding was made of Indian ricegrass, twisted or braided with the pith (central tissue) of yucca (*Yucca* sp.) leaves.

REFERENCES

Bailey, Flora, "Navajo Foods and Cooking Methods," *American Anthropologist,* 271, 287, 290.

Elmore, Francis, *Ethnobotany of the Navajo,* 26.

Franciscan Fathers, *An Ethnologic Dictionary of the Navajo Language,* 80, 190, 209, 340–41, 457.

Hocking, George M., "Some Plant Materials Used Medicinally and Otherwise by the Navaho Indians in the Chaco Canyon, New Mexico," *El Palacio,* 154.

Matthews, Washington, "Navajo Names for Plants," *The American Naturalist,* 777.

Steggerda, Morris and R. B. Eckardt, "Navajo Foods and Their Preparation," *American Dietetic Assocation Journal,* 223.

Vestal, Paul A., *Ethnobotany of the Ramah Navajo,* 16–17.

Wooten, E. O., and D. C. Stanley, *Flora of New Mexico,* 73.

Wyman, Leland, and Stuart Harris, *Navajo Indian Medical Ethnobotany,* 31, 36.

Young, Stella, *Native Plants Used by the Navajo,* 28, 71.

RUSH *(Juncus)*
wire rush

Juncus balticus Willd. ('juhn-kuss 'bawl-tik-kuss)
Juncus: Classical name for rush
balticus: Of or from the Baltic Sea

NAVAJO NAME: *Teełníyizí,* "round cattail"

DESCRIPTION & DISTRIBUTION

Wire rush is a dull green, perennial herb with slender stiff, erect stems and rhizomes (stouter horizontal subterranean stems). Heights of about 1 foot are most common, but plants as tall as 2¼ feet occur. Leaves exist merely as yellow to brown sheaths around stem bases. Flowers lack petals and appear purplish brown. Distinctions among the many rushes are slight. Flowers July through September.

Ranging from about 3,800 feet upward to about 8,000 feet, wire rush is common along washes and streams, except those rimmed with rocks, and in sporadically inundated meadows in association with other rushes, sedges (*Carex* sp.), certain grasses (Poaceae sp.), and horsetails (*Equisetum* sp.).

NAVAJO USES

MEDICINAL: This juncus is one of the emetics used for stomach troubles, skin irritations, and poisonous insect bites.

CEREMONIAL: *Teełníyizí* is used as an emetic in the five- and nine-night ceremonies.

REFERENCES

Elmore, Francis, *Ethnobotany of the Navajo,* 31.
Wyman, Leland, and Stuart Harris, *Navajo Indian Medical Ethnobotany,* 32, 37, 57–58.

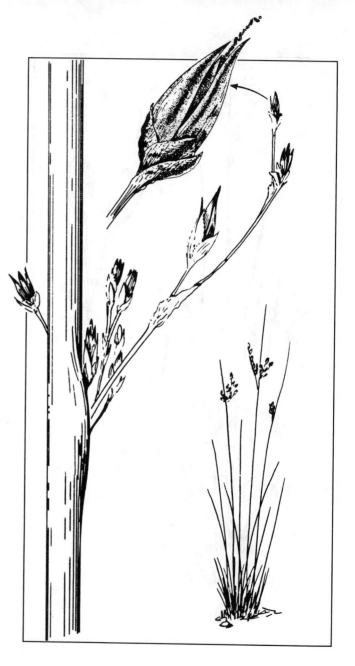

RUSSIAN THISTLE *(Salsola)*
tumbleweed, salt wort

Salsola iberica Sennen & Pau (sal-'soh-luh
　eye-'beer-ik-uh)
Salsola: From the Latin *sallere,* "to salt"
iberica: Of Spain or Portugal

NAVAJO NAME: *Ch'il deeníní,* "sharp plant"

DESCRIPTION & DISTRIBUTION
Russian thistle is an erect, densely branching olive green,
annual herb. It can grow as tall as 3 feet but usually is much
shorter, sometimes only 2 or 3 inches at maturity. Red lines
mark the stems lengthwise; both stems and linear leaves
(as long as 2 inches) are fleshy; leaves and bracts (around
the dry fruits) become spine-tipped. The so-called wing
around each fruit becomes purplish to red-purple. Russian
thistle somewhat resembles smotherweed *(Bassia
hyssopifolia),* kochia *(Kochia* sp.), and halogeton *(Halogeton
glomeratus),* which are in its family. It flowers almost
throughout the growing season from the last killing spring
frost to the first killing fall frost.

　　Russian thistle has invaded all plant communities below
about 8,000 feet elevation. It is adaptable to almost any site
where there is no competition from taller or faster growing
plants. Tolerance of adversities allows it to be a pioneer on
bare ground. Frequent associates are cheatgrass *(Bromus
tectorum)* everywhere and red brome *(Bromus rubens)* at lower
elevations.

NAVAJO USES
MEDICINAL: Russian thistle was used to treat influenza and
smallpox; the plant's ashes made a lotion and an internal
medication.

　　CEREMONIAL: *Ch'il deeníní* is used as a blackening in the
Enemy Way and Evil Way.

105

HOUSEHOLD: The fermented young plants can be made into a dull olive green dye.

When food was scarce, Navajos ate roasted Russian thistle seeds. Today, only animals eat Russian thistle, and then only when it is young or after the spines have been softened by the rain or snow.

REFERENCES

Elmore, Francis, *Ethnobotany of the Navajo*, 44.

Franciscan Fathers, *An Ethnologic Dictionary of the Navajo Language*, 181.

Hocking, George M., "Some Plant Materials Used Medicinally and Otherwise by the Navaho Indians in the Chaco Canyon, New Mexico," *El Palacio*, 155.

Martin, Neils, *Common Range Plants*, 3.

Wyman, Leland, and Stuart Harris, *Navajo Indian Medical Ethnobotany*, 24, 39.

Young, Stella, *Native Plants Used by the Navajo*, 64, 79.

SAGEBRUSH *(Artemisia)*
big sagebrush, blue sagebrush, chamiso hendiondo, common sagebrush

Artemisia tridentata Nutt. (art-em-'miz-ee-uh trye-den-'tay-ta)

Artemisia: Said to be named after Artemisia (Diana to Greeks), the Roman goddess of chastity, hunting, and the moon; also a botanist and a medical researcher who discovered several herbs

tridentata: Three-toothed, referring to the leaves

NAVAJO NAME: *Ts'ah*, "the sagebrush"

DESCRIPTION & DISTRIBUTION
Big sagebrush, an evergreen, rounded, fairly compact shrub with gray-green foliage and very small yellow flower heads in long clusters, grows to heights of about 6 feet and is aromatic. It flowers late August through early October.

Extensive stands of big sagebrush and fourwing saltbush *(Atriplex canescens)* occupy many areas between 6,500 and 7,000 feet within the range of big sagebrush from about 4,900 feet up to about 7,500 feet. Black greasewood *(Sarcobatus vermiculatus)* and fourwing saltbush; Colorado pinyon *(Pinus edulis)* and Utah juniper *(Juniperus osteosperma)*; ponderosa pine *(Pinus ponderosa)*, Colorado pinyon *(Pinus edulis)*, and Gambel oak *(Quercus gambelii)* are other communities in which big sagebrush is a prominent member, especially on medium-textured soils.

NAVAJO USES
MEDICINAL: *Artemisia tridentata* is one of the life medicines (see yarrow). Mixed with another species of sagebrush, it is said to cure headaches by odor alone. When the plant is boiled, it is said to be good for childbirth, indigestion, and constipation; a tea of the stems and leaves is said to cure colds and fevers. The tea is drunk before long hikes

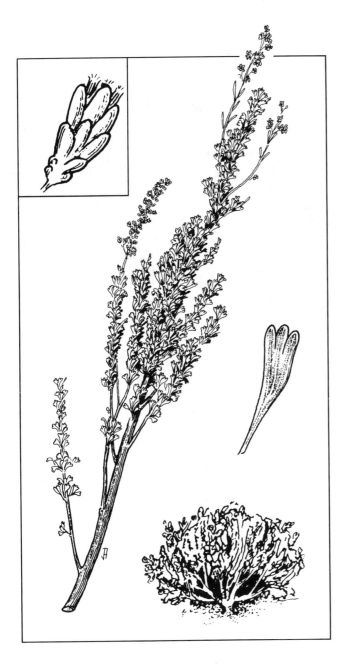

or athletic contests to "rid the body of undesirable things." A poultice made from pounded leaves is said to be good for colds, swellings, and tuberculosis or as a liniment for corns. The same medicine is used on animal sores.

CEREMONIAL: In Navajo legend, Coyote gave this tobacco to the Water Monster to calm her after he had stolen her baby. It is used in the Eagle Way, Water Way, Mountaintop Way, and Night Way. Medicine men use sagebrush as the hearth of the ceremonial firedrill. It is also a sweatbath medication.

OTHER: *Ts'ah* is used to make yellow green, and gold wool dyes.

REFERENCES

Elmore, Francis, *Ethnobotany of the Navajo,* 81.

Franciscan Fathers, *An Ethnologic Dictionary of the Navajo Language,* 114–15, 186, 257, 298.

Hocking, George M., "Some Plant Materials Used Medicinally and Otherwise by the Navaho Indians of Chaco Canyon, New Mexico," *El Palacio,* 157–58.

Martin, Neils, *Common Range Plants,* 1.

Matthews, Washington, "Navajo Names for Plants," *The American Naturalist,* 773.

Vestal, Paul A., *Ethnobotany of the Ramah Navajo,* 48.

Wyman, Leland, and Stuart Harris, *Ethnobotany of the Kayenta Navajo,* 45, 61.

Young, Stella, *Native Plants Used by the Navajo,* 52, 55, 73, 93–94.

SALTBUSH *(Atriplex)*
spiny saltbush, shadscale

Atriplex confertifolia (Torr. & Frém) Wats ('a-trih-pleks
   kon-fert-tif-'foh-lee-uh)
Atriplex: Greek for "orache," a species of this genus that
   is eaten as spinach
confertifolia: Leaves pressed close together; crowded

NAVAJO NAME: *Dá'ák'ǫ́ǫ́zh deeníní,* "sharp saltbush"

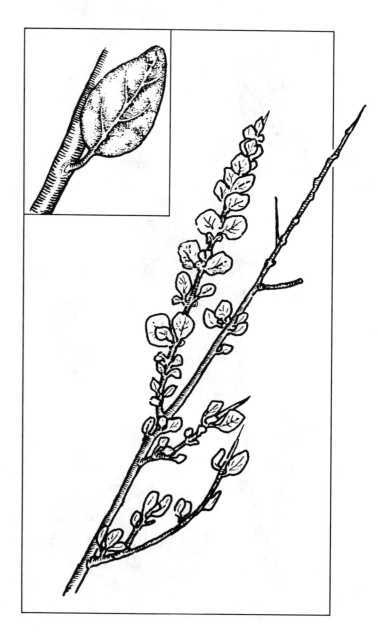

DESCRIPTION & DISTRIBUTION
Spiny saltbush is a compact, gray-green shrub about 2 feet
tall with a dense, manybranched crown. Stems change in
color from yellowish to pale gray to darker gray as they
age. Short twigs lose their leaves and become thorns. Leaves
are gray-green and shorter than ¾ inch. Inconspicuous
flowers appear in the spring.

   Below 5,500 feet elevation, spiny saltbush is prominent
in several communities: fourwing saltbush *(Atriplex
canescens)*, black greasewood *(Sarcobatus vermiculatus)*, and
spiny saltbush; spiny saltbush, Torrey joint-fir *(Ephedra
torreyana)*, and goldenweeds *(Aplopappus* sp.*)*; blackbrush
(Coleogyne ramosissima) and Torrey joint-fir. Its most
frequent associates throughout its range are other
saltbushes *(Atriplex* sp.*)*, the joint-firs *(Ephedra* sp.*)*, inland
saltgrass *(Distichlis stricta)*, and black greaseweed *(Sarcobatus
vermiculatus)*.

NAVAJO USES
HOUSEHOLD: Spiny saltbush seeds were once eaten by the
Navajo. Today, the leaves and branches are used to add a
salty flavor to corn roasted in a pit. *See appendix, page 144,
for recipe.*

   In the winter, spiny saltbush provides salt for sheep.
In the summer the plant is rubbed on horses to repel gnats.

REFERENCES

Elmore, Francis, *Ethnobotany of the Navajo*, 43.

Hocking, George M., "Some Plant Materials Used Medicinally and Otherwise by the Navaho in the Chaco Canyon, New Mexico," *El Palacio*, 149.

Kirk, Ruth F., "Navajo Bill of Fare," *New Mexico Magazine*, 16.

Wyman, Leland, and Stuart Harris, *Ethnobotany of the Kayenta Navajo*, 20.

——— , *Navajo Indian Medical Ethnobotany*, 26, 38.

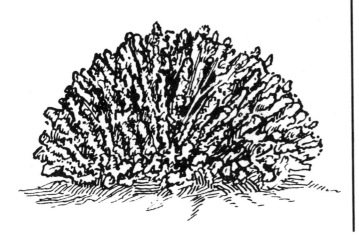

fourwing saltbush, chamiso

Atriplex canescens (Pursh) Nutt. ('a-trih-pleks kuh-'ness-senz)
canescens: Downy gray; becoming grayish

NAVAJO NAME: *Díwózhiiłbeii,* "gray greasewood"

DESCRIPTION & DISTRIBUTION

Fourwing saltbush is a fairly compact and symmetrical grayish shrub up to 6 feet tall. Pale yellow stems become tan and then gray with age. Leaves are linear to elliptical, green-gray, and as long as 2 inches but average about 1 inch. Fruits bear four "wings," which discolor from pale gray-green to yellowish to brownish as they age.

Tolerant of slightly saline and alkaline soils, fourwing saltbush associates with black greasewood *(Sarcobatus vermiculatus)* but also grows in other shrublands, woodlands, and dry, open forests. Elevational range is up to almost 7,000 feet. Other associates are big sagebrush *(Artemisia tridentata),* rubber rabbitbrush *(Chrysothamnus nauseosus),* desert wolfberry *(Lycium pallidum),* and yuccas *(Yucca* sp.).

NAVAJO USES

MEDICINAL: Fourwing saltbush is used to treat a variety of skin irritations. The leaves are chewed and used as a poultice on ant, bee, and wasp bites. A wartlike growth on chamiso is mixed with juniper mistletoe *(Phoradendron juniperinum)* and used to treat toothaches and stomachaches. The same mixture can be taken during a sweatbath to increase perspiration. Chamiso leaves and roots can be made into a cough medicine. The plant can also be used as snuff to relieve nasal problems.

CEREMONIAL: *Díwózhiiłbeii* is used as an emetic in Evil Way and Navajo Wind Way ceremonies.

OTHER: Chamiso was used for food. The leaves give a salty flavor to corn roasting in a pit. The seeds were parched and ground into a meal, which could be used alone or added

109

to other flour. Flowers were added to puddings. Navajo livestock eat *díwózhiilbeii* in winter and early spring when other foliage is scarce. A mixture of chamiso and juniper (*Juniperus* sp.) twigs is used to treat sheep who bloat from eating chamiso in warm weather. The ashes of the leaves and twigs are rubbed on the scalp for a hair tonic.

Fourwing saltbush has several dye uses. The leaves and twigs make a yellow dye, with raw alum (aluminum sulfate; found at the base of rock cliffs on the reservation) used as the mordant. Ashes of the leaves and twigs are added to red buckskin dye to intensify the color.

REFERENCES

Elmore, Francis, *Ethnobotany of the Navajo,* 43.

Hocking, George M., "Some Plant Materials Used Medicinally and Otherwise by the Navaho Indians in the Chaco Canyon, New Mexico," *El Palacio,* 148, 149.

Martin, Neils, *Common Range Plants,* 2.

Vestal, Paul A., *Ethnobotany of the Ramah Navajo,* 24.

Wyman, Leland, and Stuart Harris, *Ethnobotany of the Kayenta Navajo,* 20.

Young, Stella, *Native Plants Used by the Navajo,* 47–72.

SANDPUFF *(Tripterocalyx)*
Wooton sandpuff, common sandpuff

Tripterocalyx carnea (Greene) Galloway
    (trip-tuhr-row-'kay-liks karn-'ee-uh)
Tripterocalyx: "Three-wing calyx," referring to the
             "wings," or appendages, on the fruit
carnea: Flesh color

NAVAJO NAME: *Tl'ohchin nilchiin,* "smelly onion"

DESCRIPTION & DISTRIBUTION
Wooton sandpuff—one of the several relatives of wild four
o'clock—is a semiprostrate, annual herb with fleshy
greenish to purplish stems bearing thick paired leaves and
clusters of slender, white and pink flowers. It seldom
reaches a height of more than 6 inches, but some stems may
be as long as 15 inches. Small-flowered sandpuff
(Tripterocalyx micranthus) is another local species in the same
genus. Flowers mid-May through early September.

    Coarse soils (from sandy loams to loose, sandy soils)
in basins, along roadsides and shores, and around bases of
dunes in shrublands and in woodlands below 7,000 feet are
common sites for wooton sandpuff. Associated with
Wooton sandpuff are small-flowered sandpuff, sand
verbena *(Abronia* sp.), Indian ricegrass *(Oryzopsis
hymenoides),* dropseed *(Sporobolus* sp.), and evening primrose
(Oenothera sp.).

NAVAJO USES
MEDICINAL: A medicine is made from the plant to treat
internal injuries, such as those caused by a fall. Wooton
sandpuff can be used for gallbladder or gallstone problems;
it is made into a tea.

    OTHER: It was said to be a goodluck plant and is carried
for protection.

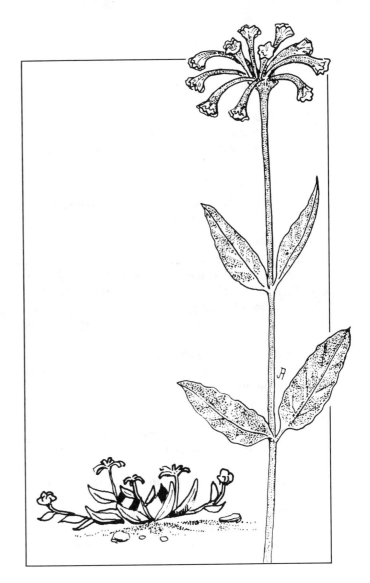

REFERENCES
Vestal, Paul A., *Ethnobotany of the Ramah Navajo,* 26.

SCRAMBLED EGGS *(Corydalis)*
golden smoke, mountain corydalis

Corydalis aurea Willd. (coh-'rid-al-iss 'aw-ree-uh)
Corydalis: Named after the crested lark (from the Greek
korudallis) for its spur, which is suggested
by the flower
aurea: Golden

NAVAJO NAME: *Ṭazhii yilchiin áłts'íísígíí,* "little turkey-like
odor"

DESCRIPTION & DISTRIBUTION
Golden smoke is an attractive but relatively inconspicuous
biennial or perennial herb with olive green stems and leaves
and yellowish, irregular asymmetrical flowers. The plant
is hairless, somewhat waxy, and up to 1 foot tall. Stems turn
yellowish with age. Pods are about 1 inch long. Flowers
from April through June.

Mountain corydalis is almost rare throughout its fairly
wide range, below 7,000 feet elevation on coarse soils of
roadsides and other disturbed sites.

NAVAJO USES
MEDICINAL: Golden smoke is used to treat diarrhea,
rheumatism, arthritis, snakebite, injuries, sorethroat,
stomachache, and backache.

CEREMONIAL: *Ṭazhii yilchiin áłts'íísígíí* ashes were used
for blackening in a now obsolete ceremony, the Raven Way.

OTHER: Watermelon seeds are soaked in an infusion of
Corydalis aurea before planting to increase the yield. Golden
smoke can be sprinkled on livestock to keep snakes away.

REFERENCES

Elmore, Francis, *Ethnobotany of the Navajo,* 48.
Franciscan Fathers, *An Ethnologic Dictionary of the Navajo Language,* 114, 189.
Vestal, Paul A., *Ethnobotany of the Ramah Navajo,* 28.
Wyman, Leland, and Stuart Harris, *Ethnobotany of the Kayenta Navajo,* 23, 62.
———— , *Navajo Indian Medical Ethnobotany,* 23, 27, 40, 58–59, 62.
Young, Stella, *Native Plants Used by the Navajo,* 86.

SERVICEBERRY *(Amelanchier)*
Utah serviceberry, shadbush, Juneberry

Amelanchier utahensis Koehne (a-meh-'lan-kih-err yew-taw-'en-siss)
Amelanchier: French name for a related European species, the medlar-tree, whose fruit was eaten when decayed
utahensis: Of or from Utah

NAVAJO NAME: *Didzédit'ódii,* "soft fruit"

DESCRIPTION & DISTRIBUTION

Utah serviceberry is a large deciduous shrub attaining heights up to about 12 feet. Twigs are reddish brown; branchlets are gray-brown; branches are grayish. Leaves resemble those of common mountain mahogany *(Cercocarpus montanus)* but are thinner, toothed not as far down the sides, and scarcely hairy. Small fruits (less than ⅜ inch across) are dark purplish to violet. White flowers bloom May through June.

Between elevations of 3,800 feet and 9,000 feet, Utah serviceberry is a member of various shrub, woodland, and forest communities, often on coarse soils of rocky or stony hillsides. At low elevations it may grow near waterways; at high elevations southslopes are common places. Its associates include common cliffrose *(Cowania mexicana),* junipers *(Juniperus* sp.), big sagebrush *(Artemisia tridentata),* common mountain mahogany *(Cercocarpus montanus),* cliff fendlerbush *(Fendlera rupicola),* and Gambel oak *(Quercus gambelii),* depending upon elevation.

NAVAJO USES

MEDICINAL: Serviceberry is one of the life medicines (see yarrow); its leaves have an emetic action. Navajos use emetics to treat nausea, stomach problems, animal bites, and skin irritations. It is used in childbirth.

113

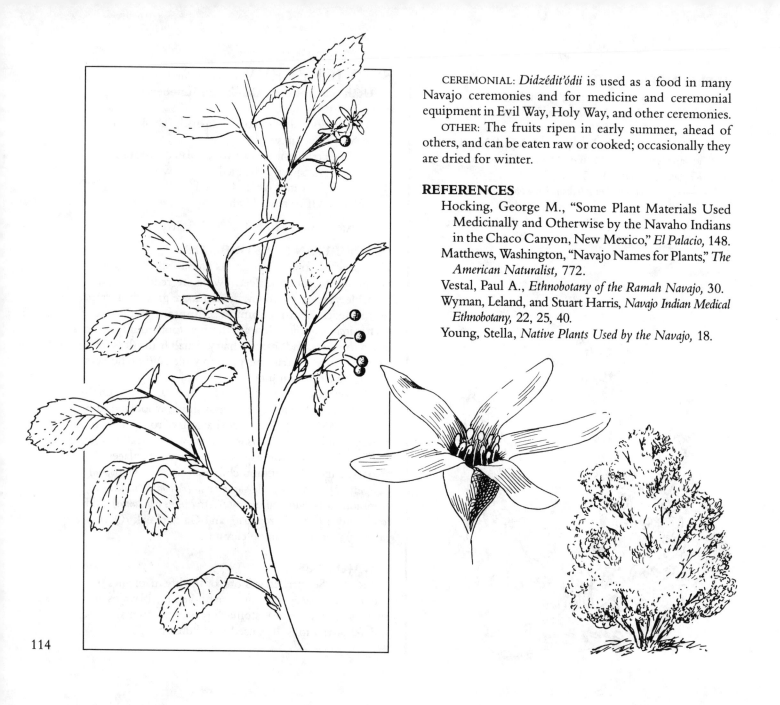

CEREMONIAL: *Didzédit'ódii* is used as a food in many Navajo ceremonies and for medicine and ceremonial equipment in Evil Way, Holy Way, and other ceremonies.

OTHER: The fruits ripen in early summer, ahead of others, and can be eaten raw or cooked; occasionally they are dried for winter.

REFERENCES

Hocking, George M., "Some Plant Materials Used Medicinally and Otherwise by the Navaho Indians in the Chaco Canyon, New Mexico," *El Palacio,* 148.

Matthews, Washington, "Navajo Names for Plants," *The American Naturalist,* 772.

Vestal, Paul A., *Ethnobotany of the Ramah Navajo,* 30.

Wyman, Leland, and Stuart Harris, *Navajo Indian Medical Ethnobotany,* 22, 25, 40.

Young, Stella, *Native Plants Used by the Navajo,* 18.

SNAKEWEED *(Gutierrezia)*
broom snakeweed, brownweed, matchweed, sheepweed, yellowweed

Gutierrezia sarothrae (Pursh) Britt. and Rusby
   (goo-tih-ehr-'ree-zih-uh suh-'roh-three)
Gutierrezia: Named for Pedro Gutierrez, a correspondent of the Botanic Garden, Madrid, Spain
sarothrae: Greek for "broom," especially a broom made of twigs

NAVAJO NAME: *Ch'il diilyésiitsoh,* "big dodge weed"

DESCRIPTION & DISTRIBUTION

Broom snakeweed is a small shrub with a very dense crown. Height seldom exceeds 1½ feet. Young stems are greenish, later tan, eventually gray-brown. The linear leaves are green and up to 1½ inches long. Rays of the many small heads are yellow. Broom snakeweed resembles small-flowered snakeweed *(Gutierrezia microcephala)* and Greene rabbitbrush *(Chrysothamnus greenei);* however, the heads of small-flowered snakeweed are not as large as those of broom snakeweed, and the stems of Greene rabbitbrush change from greenish to whitish to grayish as they age, while the heads are rayless. Flowers July through September.

Broom snakeweed may cover more acres than any other perennial plant in Navajoland. Between elevations of about 3,800 and 7,500 feet, it is a major constituent of most shrubland and woodland communities and is fairly common in the drier forest. Among its frequent associates are small-flowered snakeweed *(Gutierrezia microcephala),* Greene rabbitbrush, other rabbitbrushes *(Chrysothamnus* sp.), manyflowered baby-aster *(Leucelene ericoides),* and various golden weeds *(Aplopappus* sp.).

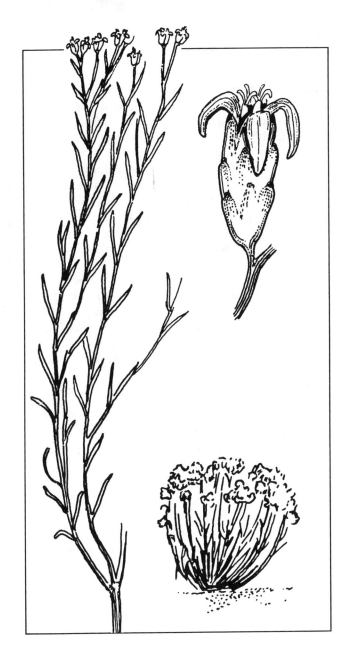

NAVAJO USES

MEDICINAL: Snakeweed is used to heal cuts and bites in humans and animals. The plant is chewed and the pulp placed on the bite of an ant, bee, or wasp. It is used to heal castration incisions in livestock. To treat snakebite in sheep, the plant is boiled, then placed on the bite. The swelling is said to go down immediately.

Snakeweed medicine is given in childbirth.

The ashes of this and other plants are rubbed on the forehead to cure a headache, nervousness, or fever.

The root is used to treat stomachache and other internal problems. Snakeweed is not only one of the life medicines (see yarrow), it is used as an antidote for taking too much life medicine.

CEREMONIAL: *Ch'il diilyésiitsoh* is used in almost every ceremony. The plant is burned and mixed with other plants and minerals to make a blackening for the Evil Way, Holy Way, and Handtrembling Way. It is used to make Enemy Way unravelers and prayersticks and Chiricahua Wind Way prayersticks. It is used as a ceremonial emetic and fumigent.

It is a Life Way pollen.

OTHER: The flowers make a yellow dye. The stems can be used to make fire by friction.

REFERENCES

Hocking, George M., "Some Plant Materials Used Medicinally and Otherwise by the Navaho Indians in the Chaco Canyon, New Mexico," *El Palacio*, 151.

Matthews, Washington, "Navajo Names for Plants," *The American Naturalist*, 773.

Vestal, Paul A., *Ethnobotany of the Ramah Navajo*, 51.

Wyman, Leland, and Stuart Harris, *Ethnobotany of the Kayenta Navajo*, 48, 62.

——— , *Navajo Indian Medical Ethnobotany*, 24, 29, 47, 57–58, 62, 65, 67–69, 73–74.

Young, Stella, *Native Plants Used by the Navajo*, 87.

SOAPWEED *(Yucca)*
narrowleaf yucca, fineleaf yucca, bear grass, mesa yucca, Indian cabbage, pamilla

Yucca angustissima Engelm ('yuk-kuh an-gus-'tih-sih-muh)

Yucca: Named after the root of the cassava plant from which tapioca is made (yucca is a Carib word), perhaps because of the similarity of the roots
angustissima: Narrow-leafed

NAVAJO NAMES: *Tsá'ászi'ts'óóz,* "narrow yucca" (*Talawosh,* "water suds," name for root; *Nidoodloho,* "the green fruit"; *Nideeshjiin,* "stalk black," name for young, dark stalk; *Nideesgai,* "stalk white," name for taller stalk)

DESCRIPTION & DISTRIBUTION

Fineleaf yucca is a perennial with fleshy, long, stiff, narrow, pointed leaves and a tall stalk of large, white flowers growing almost directly from the fleshy roots. Leaves may extend 20 inches above the root crown. The flowering stalk may reach 4 feet. The fruit is a large, plump capsule with many medium seeds; the capsule becomes woody and splits open.

Conspicuous but scattered, these yuccas occur across the reservation in communities of blackbrush (*Coleogyne ramosissima*) and joint-fir (*Ephedra* sp.), shadscale (*Atriplex confertifolia*) and black greasewood (*Sarcobatus vermiculatus*), big sagebrush (*Artemisia tridentata*) and fourwing saltbush (*Atriplex canescens*), blue grama (*Bouteloua gracilis*) and galleta (*Hilaria jamesii*), Colorado pinyon (*Pinus edulis*) and junipers (*Juniperus* sp.), and ponderosa pine (*Pinus ponderosa*) and Gambel oak (*Quercus gambelii*). Elevations are from about 3,800 feet to about 7,000 feet. Associates are green Mormon tea (*Ephedra viridis*), sand dropseed (*Sporobolus cryptandrus*), broom snakeweed (*Gutierrezia sarothræ*), and Greene

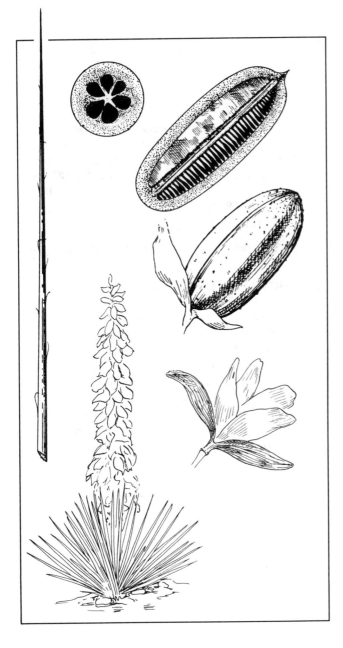

rabbitbrush *(Chrysothamnus greenei)*. The sites are often slopes with coarse to medium soils.

NAVAJO USES

CEREMONIAL: Fiber from the narrowleaf yucca is used to tie ceremonial equipment—hoops, prayersticks, unravelers, and chant arrows. The juice is used to make paint for ceremonial pipes. Leaves of a yucca that a deer has jumped over are heated in coals. When they are soft, juice is wrung from the leaves onto small flat stones that hold paint pigments.

Probably the most important ceremonial use of *tsá'ászi'ts'óóz* is bathing in suds made from yucca root. For example, boys and girls have their hair washed with yucca suds on the next to the last night of the Nightway. Most ceremonies include a ceremonial bath of yucca suds for the patients as well as the singer, along with other cleansing rituals. Purification, clean thinking, and a serious attitude are important in Navajo ceremonies.

Navajo creation stories tell how the Navajos learned weaving from Spider Woman, a Navajo holy person. Before the 1500s, Navajos wove mats and sandals with fiber from the narrowleaf yucca, the inner bark of the juniper (*Juniperus* sp.), and later, with locally grown cotton. All this changed when the Navajos acquired sheep from the Spaniards.

MEDICINAL: *Yucca angustissima* is used in childbirth. The roots are soaked in water, the liquid strained and given to a woman having a long labor. A cupful of yucca suds and sugar is given to the mother to help deliver the afterbirth.

OTHER: Yucca is used to wash wool and as an ingredient in several dyes. Soap made from the crushed root of this or *Yucca baccata* is used to wash hair. Sometimes sagebrush (*Artemisia* sp.) is added to make the hair smell good, grow long and soft, and to prevent it from falling out.

The 102 counters in the Moccasin Game are often made of *Yucca angustissima*. An arrow poison is made with yucca

117

juice mixed with charcoal from a lightning-struck pinyon (*Pinus* sp.) or juniper (*Juniperus* sp.) tree and rubbed on 6 inches of the tip of the arrow.

This yucca is often called the banana plant by Navajos, although the fruit tastes more like a date and is not considered as good to eat as the fruit of the wideleaf yucca (*Yucca baccata*). However, the fruit may be roasted in ashes, eaten raw, or sliced and dried for winter.

The crushed fruit is used to make a cheese from goat's milk.

Other parts of the plant are edible. Flower buds are roasted in ashes for 15 minutes; leaves are boiled with salt.

Sheep also eat yucca, especially the flower buds.

REFERENCES

Bailey, Flora, "Navajo Foods and Cooking Methods," *American Anthropologist*, 286.

Darby, William J., et al., "A Study of the Dietary Background and Nutriture of the Navajo Indian," *The Journal of Nutrition*, 21–22.

Elmore, Francis, *Ethnobotany of the Navajo*, 33–34.

Franciscan Fathers, *An Ethnologic Dictionary of the Navajo Language*, 194, 371–73, 417–18.

Hocking, George M., "Some Plant Materials Used Medicinally and Otherwise by the Navaho Indians in the Chaco Canyon, New Mexico," *El Palacio*, 164.

Kluckhohn, Clyde, and Dorothea Leighton, *The Navajo*, 207, 218.

Matthews, Washington, "Navajo Names for Plants," *The American Naturalist*, 777.

Vestal, Paul A., *Ethnobotany of the Ramah Navajo*, 21.

Wyman, Leland, and Stuart Harris, *Navajo Indian Medical Ethnobotany*, 21, 37, 53.

Young, Stella, *Native Plants Used by the Navajo*, 22, 35–36, 39.

SPECTACLEPOD (*Dimorphocarpa*)
common spectaclepod

Dimorphocarpa wislizeni (Engelm) Rollins
    (dye-more-foe-'car-puh wiss-lih-'zee-neye)
Dimorphocarpa: From the Greek *di*, "two," *morpho*, "shaped," and *carpa*, "seedpods"
wislizeni: Named for German-born physician and naturalist, Frederick A. Wislizenus (1810–99), later of St. Louis, who collected plants in the 1840s and 1850s in the southwestern United States and Mexico

NAVAJO NAME: *Nahasht'e'iidą́ą́' łibahígíí*, "gray kangaroo rat food"

DESCRIPTION & DISTRIBUTION

Common spectaclepod is an erect, gray-green annual herb with 1 to several stems bearing toothed leaves and clusters of small, white flowers. It may grow as tall as 1 foot with leaves as long as 2¼ inches, but it is usually smaller. The flattened fruit and 2 side-by-side seeds resemble eyeglasses. Flowers early April through early October.

Embankments, roadsides, and gully edges of mostly coarse soils between elevations of about 4,000 and 6,800 feet are frequently occupied by scattered plants of this species, usually with few other associates.

NAVAJO USES

MEDICINAL: Spectaclepod is used as an internal and external medication for venereal diseases. It is also used to treat itchy or irritated skin: chicken pox, measles, cold sores, sunburn, and insect bites. Parents have children chew the plant to strengthen their teeth.

CEREMONIAL: *Nahasht'e'iidą́ą́' łibahígíí* is used in the Beauty Way, Water Way, Hail Way, and Mountaintop Way ceremonies.

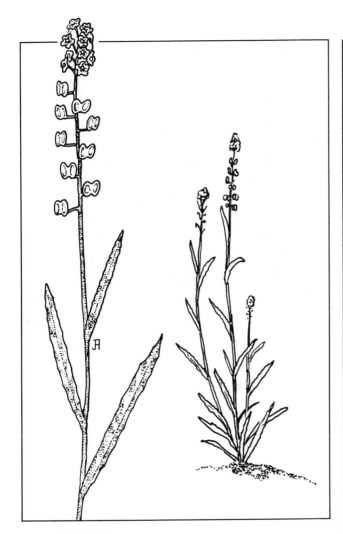

REFERENCES
Elmore, Francis, *Ethnobotany of the Navajo*, 49.
Vestal, Paul A., *Ethnobotany of the Ramah Navajo*, 28.
Wyman, Leland, and Stuart Harris, *Ethnobotany of the Kayenta Navajo*, 24, 61.

SPIDERWORT *(Tradescantia)*
prairie spiderwort

Tradescantia occidentalis (Britt.) Smyth.
    (trad-ees-'kan-shee-uh ok-si-den-'tay-liss)
Tradescantia: Named after an Englishman, John Tradescant
    (1608–62), gardener to King Charles I,
    who visited the Virginia colony in 1654
occidentalis: Of the western world

NAVAJO NAME: *Áłtsíní Iilt'ąą'í*, "mariposa-like leaf"

DESCRIPTION & DISTRIBUTION
Prairie spiderwort is an herbaceous perennial with dull green, grasslike stems and leaves, and with clusters of indigo to violet flowers. It resembles members of the lily family. Height is under 2 feet. Flowers April through August.

Individual plants are scattered in fairly dense vegetation below 7,000 feet on moist soils.

NAVAJO USES
MEDICINAL: The spiderwort root is used for internal injuries.

CEREMONIAL: Prairie spiderwort is a medicine used in the Night Way.

REFERENCES
Vestal, Paul A., *Ethnobotany of the Ramah Navajo*, 20.
Wyman, Leland, and Stuart Harris, *Ethnobotany of the Kayenta Navajo*, 16.
——— , *Navajo Indian Medical Ethnobotany*, 28, 37.

SPURGE *(Euphorbia)*
Fendler spurge

Euphorbia fendleri T. & G. (you-'for-bee-uh 'fend-lurr-eye)

Euphorbia: Named for Euphorbus, a Greek physician of the first century

fendleri: Named for August Fendler (1813–83), German born naturalist and explorer, who was one of the first botanists to collect plants in New Mexico, Texas, and Venezuela

NAVAJO NAME: *Ch'il abe'é yázhí,* "little milkweed"

DESCRIPTION & DISTRIBUTION

Fendler spurge is a tiny, perennial herb with several semiprostrate, reddish stems and unusual, minute flowers with a periphery of pinkish spots bordered with white petallike parts. The plant is inconspicuous. Flowers May through July.

Disturbed areas of coarse to medium soil around depressions and along rills below 7,000 feet may be temporarily occupied by Fendler spurge until it is displaced by other weeds.

NAVAJO USES

MEDICINAL: Fendler spurge has a milky sap and is used by nursing mothers to increase their milk supply and for breast injuries. It is also used to treat indigestion, diarrhea, and snakebite in humans and animals and skin irritations such as poison ivy, warts, boils, and pimples. It is said to be hemostatic.

CEREMONIAL: *Ch'il abe'é yázhí* is used as a Beauty Way medicine.

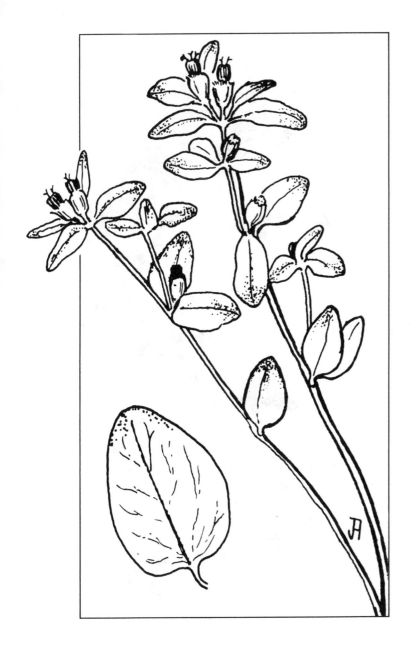

REFERENCES

Franciscan Fathers, *An Ethnologic Dictionary of the Navajo Language,* 115–16, 189.

Hocking, George M., "Some Plant Materials Used Medicinally and Otherwise by the Navaho Indians in the Chaco Canyon, New Mexico," *El Palacio,* 151.

Vestal, Paul A., *Ethnobotany of the Ramah Navajo,* 35.

Wyman, Leland, and Stuart Harris, *Navajo Indian Medical Ethnobotany,* 23, 56, 66.

Young, Stella, *Native Plants Used by the Navajo,* 86, 96.

SUMAC *(Rhus)*
skunkbush, three-leaved sumac, squawberry, lemonadeberry

Rhus trilobata Nutt. ('russ try-loh-'bay-tuh)
Rhus: Ancient Greek and Latin name for a European
     tree of the same genus; from the Greek *rhodos,*
     "red," for the fruit
trilobata: Describes the shape of the leaves; *tri,* "three,"
     lobatus, "having small projections or lobes"

NAVAJO NAME: *K'įį*, "sumac"

DESCRIPTION & DISTRIBUTION

Skunkbush is an irregularly branching, sprawling shrub
somewhat malodorous and seldom exceeding 5 feet in
height. Young twigs are very flexible, resilient, and pale
brown, becoming gray, while older stems are more rigid
and brownish. Leaves are green and shiny; their stems are
purplish or blue-red. Small, yellowish flowers produce
orange-red berries about ⅓ inch in diameter. Flowers April
through May.

Skunkbush is distributed from the lowest parts of the
reservation up to elevations of about 7,500 feet, nestled
beside boulders, on talus (rock slides), in canyons, on rocky
banks of washes, and along streams. Scattered through
shrubland, woodland, and forest, its most common
associates may be Utah serviceberry *(Amelanchier utahensis),*
cliff fendlerbush *(Fendlera rupicola),* and cliffrose *(Cowania
mexicana).*

NAVAJO USES

MEDICINAL: Leaves are used to treat skin problems, such as
poison ivy, dermatitis, or itching; stomach problems; and
are used in childbirth and as a contraceptive.

A treatment for falling hair was made from the oil of the
fruits. The berries were boiled and the oil that rose to the
top of the pan was skimmed off and rubbed into the scalp.

122

HOUSEHOLD: The red berries are used for food. They can be eaten raw, cooked, or dried and stored for winter. A soup is made by grinding the raw berries, mixing them with a small amount of flour and cornmeal, and adding that mixture to boiling water. The soup is boiled for ten minutes; sugar is added before serving. The berries are also cooked with meat or roasted corn or used raw in a "lemonade."

Sumac is used for wool and basketry dyes as a dye mordant and for the sticks to stir the dye. A black dye for baskets and leather is made from the leaves, branches, or twigs of *Rhus trilobata*, ochre, and pinyon (*Pinus* sp.) pitch.

An orange-brown dye is made from the fermented berries, and a blue dye is made from sumac boiled with a pulverized blue clay. The ashes are used as a mordant for wool and basketry dyes.

Navajo baskets, including the ceremonial basket (Fig. 1) called a "wedding basket" (because a new basket is used in the Navajo wedding ceremony and is a gift to the groom's mother afterward) and other baskets not often seen today, are made of sumac.

One, used for carrying or storing water (Fig. 2) was made in the shape of a large jar with handles of braided horsehair attached to the sides. It was given a glasslike finish by coating it inside and out with boiling pinyon (*Pinus* sp.) pitch.

The sumac is tied, as it is gathered, with yucca (*Yucca* sp.) fiber, never string. The sumac twigs used for baskets are torn into three strips; then the bark is removed. After some of the strips are dyed, often using a dye containing sumac, both the natural and dyed strips are soaked in water to make them flexible.

The end of a strip that grew closest to the ground is wound around a small stick and tied with yucca to make the base of the basket. Next, yucca is sewn sunwise, left to right, around the sumac coils with a deer-bone awl.

A good basket will hold water after a few minutes of moistening.

CEREMONIAL: Sumac pollen is required for some ceremonies. Several ceremonial items in the Night Way, Chiricahua Wind Way, Evil Way, and Mountain Chants are made from sumac.

The stories say *k'įį'* was given to the Navajos by the bat.

REFERENCES

Elmore, Francis, *Ethnobotany of the Navajo*, 60–61.
Franciscan Fathers, *An Ethnologic Dictionary of the Navajo Language*, 181–82, 211, 230, 232, 245, 292–96, 303–204, 318, 400, 405, 416–17, 495.
Kluckhohn, Clyde, et al., *Navajo Material Culture*, 107–108, 134, 337–38.
Stephen, A. M., "The Navajo," *American Anthropologist*, 345, 348, 358, 362.
Vestal, Paul A., *Ethnobotany of the Ramah Navajo*, 35.
Wyman, Leland, and Stuart Harris, *Ethnobotany of the Kayenta Navajo*, 31.
———, *Navajo Indian Medical Ethnobotany*, 23, 42, 73.
Young, Stella, *Native Plants Used by the Navajo*, 19, 37, 42.

Fig. 2

Fig. 1

SUNFLOWER (Helianthus)
annual sunflower, common sunflower

Helianthus annuus L. (he-lee-'an-thus an-'new-uus)
Helianthus: From the Greek *helios,* "sun," and *anthus,*
"flower"
annuus: From the Latin *annuum,* "year"

NAVAJO NAME: *Nidíyíliitsoh,* "big sunflower"

DESCRIPTION & DISTRIBUTION

Annual sunflower is a tall, erect, annual herb with bristly
stems and leaves. It may attain 5 feet in height with 5-inch
leaves and 4-inch flower heads with a central brownish disk
and radiating yellow rays. Prairie sunflower *(Helianthus
petiolaris)* is similar but smaller. Flowers June through early September.

In association with prairie sunflower, common
cocklebur *(Xanthium strumarium),* small-flowered gaura
(Gaura parviflora), and golden crownbeard *(Verbesina
encelioides),* it occupies soils of medium and fine textures
along highways, around irrigated fields, in basins, and in
areas with extra water and some soil disturbance; on coarser
soils it grows with Rocky Mountain beeplant *(Cleome serrulata),* prairie sunflower *(Helianthus petiolaris),* and Texas
doveweed *(Croton texensis)* along washes and roadsides.
Below 6,900 feet, it is widely distributed but only locally
abundant.

NAVAJO USES

MEDICINAL: Sunflowers are used to treat prenatal infection.

To remove a wart, sunflower stalk pith (central tissue
of the stem) is burned and the powder placed on the wart.

HOUSEHOLD: Sunflowers were a major food before the
arrival of beans, corn, and squash from Mexico. Sunflower
seeds have been cultivated for at least 3,000 years. Navajos
used the seeds alone or mixed with corn. The seeds were
ground into meal and made into cakes, bread, or dump-

lings boiled in goat's milk or water. Sunflower seeds were said to improve the appetite. *See appendix, page 144, for nutritional composition.*

The hull (outer seed covering) is boiled to make a dull dark red dye.

The hollow stalks were used to make a bird snare.

CEREMONIAL: A flute with four notes made from a common sunflower stalk is used to time the grinding of the corn in the Enemy Way.

Nidíyíliitsoh is used in medicine for the Enemy Way, Mountain Chant, and Night Way and in sandpaintings.

REFERENCES

Dodge, Natt, *100 Roadside Wildflowers of the Southwest Uplands*, 83.

Elmore, Francis, *Ethnobotany of the Navajo*, 87.

Hocking, George M., "Some Plant Materials Used Medicinally and Otherwise by the Navaho Indians in the Chaco Canyon, New Mexico," *El Palacio*, 152.

Steggerda, Morris, and R. B. Eckardt, "Navajo Foods and Their Preparation," *American Dietetic Association Journal*, 223.

Vestal, Paul A., *Ethnobotany of the Ramah Navajo*, 51.

Wyman, Leland, and Stuart Harris, *Ethnobotany of the Kayenta Navajo*, 48, 62.

———, *Navajo Indian Medical Ethnobotany*, 31, 47, 65, 72.

Young, Stella, *Native Plants Used by the Navajo*, 31.

SWEET-CLOVER *(Melilotus)*
yellow sweet-clover

Melilotus officinalis (L.) Lam. (mel-il-'loh-tus off-iss-in-'nay-liss)

Melilotus: "Honey lotus," for the scent which is attractive to bees

officinalis: Originally, "of shop," or "apothecary," then "officinal." Recognized in the *Pharmacopoeia* (a book containing information on the preparation and use of recognized drugs)

NAVAJO NAME: *Azeets'óóz*, "slender medicine"

DESCRIPTION & DISTRIBUTION

Yellow sweet-clover is an herbaceous biennial almost indistinguishable from white sweet-clover *(Melilotus albus)*, except in flower color, and superficially resembling the medics *(Medicago* sp.) and some true clovers *(Trifolium* sp.). One to several stems grow up to 3 feet tall from the root-crown. Each leaf has 3 leaflets, as do those of the medics and clovers. It has ¼-inch, yellow flowers in racemes (long, slender clusters). Pods are small and fairly smooth (those of white sweet-clover may be transversely wrinkled). Flowers from late May through August and probably into September.

The sweet-clovers require copious precipitation or periodic, brief flooding. They grow along roadsides (benefitting from the extra runoff) in the higher woodlands and lower forests and around irrigated fields and along washes in the shrublands. The elevational range is up to 7,000 feet. Associates are sunflowers *(Helianthus* sp.), Russian knapweed *(Centaurea repens)*, pigweeds *(Amaranthus* sp.), Rocky Mountain beeplant *(Cleome serrulata)*, common cocklebur *(Xanthium strumarium)*, and some of the erect knotweeds *(Polygonum* sp.).

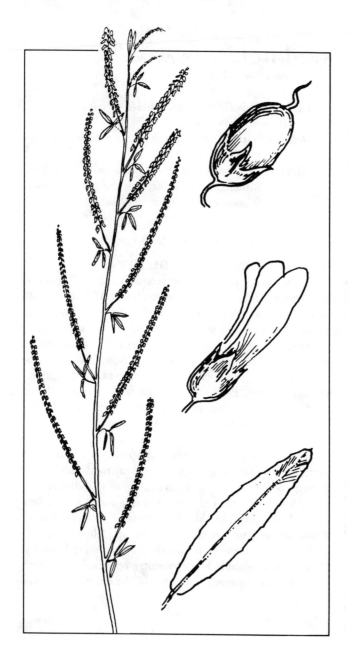

NAVAJO USES

MEDICINAL: The plant is made into a liquid to be drunk or rubbed on the body to treat colds.

OTHER: It is eaten by livestock.

REFERENCES

Elmore, Francis, *Ethnobotany of the Navajo*, 57.
Vestal, Paul A., *Ethnobotany of the Ramah Navajo*, 33.

TAMARISK *(Tamarix)*
French tamarisk

Tamarix chinensis Loureiro ('tam-ar-ix chin-'nen-siss)
Tamarix: Classical name, possibly from the Tamaris
       River in Spain, where it was said to grow
chinensis: Of China

NAVAJO NAME: *Gad ni'eełii bílátah łichí'ígíí,* "Rocky
       Mountain juniper with red flowers"

DESCRIPTION & DISTRIBUTION
French tamarisk is a large, many-stemmed shrub sometimes 12 feet tall. Foliage resembles that of juniper (*Juniperus*
sp.) but is finer. Young shoots are greenish, becoming red-
brown as twigs, and darker as branches. The minute flowers
are pink and appear from late May through August.

    Ranging from about 6,400 feet down to the lowest ele-
vations of Navajoland, French tamarisk is replacing
willows along lake and stream shores and in washes. Its
associates are Russian olive *(Elaeagnus angustifolia)* and various willows (*Salix* sp.).

NAVAJO USES
MEDICINAL: French tamarisk is soaked in water and drunk
for a variety of illnesses or used for a smoke treatment, often
as a substitute for juniper (*Juniperus* sp.).

    OTHER: French tamarisk was introduced by the
Spaniards for shade and erosion control. Thus, it does not
fit into the Navajo mythology in which plants originally
within or on the Navajos' sacred mountains are mentioned
in Navajo stories and have specific uses in Navajo culture.
However, because it resembles the juniper, it is gradually
being used like juniper; for instance for heald sticks used
in weaving.

REFERENCES
Elmore, Francis, *Ethnobotany of the Navajo,* 63.
Hocking, George M., "Some Plant Materials Used
    Medicinally and Otherwise by the Navaho Indians in
    the Chaco Canyon, New Mexico," *El Palacio,* 163.

THREE-AWN *(Aristida)*
purple three-awn, wire grass

Aristida purpurea Nutt. (ar-'riss-tih-da pur'-pew-ree-uh)
Aristida: Aris refers to the unique awn
purpurea: Purple

NAVAJO NAME: *Dlǫ́ǫ́'bibé'ézhóó',* "prairie-dog comb"

DESCRIPTION & DISTRIBUTION
Purple three-awn is a short (usually under 10 inches), perennial bunch grass with fine, inrolled, curly leaves that are exceeded in height by the cluster of spikelets. Awns of the spikelets are about 1½ inches long. It flowers April through June.

At elevations under about 7,300 feet, purple three-awn is a constituent of a variety of plant communities. Often it grows on soils of coarse to medium textures and is most abundant in the Colorado pinyon *(Pinus edulis)* and Utah juniper *(Juniperus osteosperma)* community.

NAVAJO USES
CEREMONIAL: *Dlǫ́ǫ́ bibé'ézhóó'* is mixed with other plants and is used as a medicine in the Enemy Way.

OTHER: The Navajo name for wire grass mentions a comb, and the literature records that it was used for a hairbrush.

REFERENCES
Franciscan Fathers, *An Ethnologic Dictionary of the Navajo Language,* 190.
Personal communications, July 1979.
Vestal, Paul A., *Ethnobotany of the Ramah Navajo,* 15.

TOWNSENDIA *(Townsendia)*
hoary ground-daisy, Easter-daisy

Townsendia incana Nutt. (town-'sen-dee-uh in-'kay-nuh)

Townsendia: Named for David Townsend (1787–1858),
Pennsylvania banker, botanist, and plant
collector

incana: From the Latin *hoary,* "covered with gray or
white hairs"; on this plant, the hoary growth is
on the stem.

NAVAJO NAME: *Azee' ná'ołtá adiitsoh,* "big unwinding
medicine"

DESCRIPTION & DISTRIBUTION

Hoary ground-daisy is short (under 6 inches, usually), herbaceous, and probably perennial with fuzzy, gray-green
stems and leaves. There may be several flower heads with
orange centers and whitish to pale bluish rays; the heads
appear large relative to the diminutive size of the plant.
Flowers from sometime in April through summer.

This little herb occurs sparsely throughout the reservation below 7,500 feet, but is most common — and even
then scattered in woodlands and forests — between 6,400
and 7,000 feet in sites of fairly coarse and stony soils with
appreciable litter (plant debris).

NAVAJO USES

MEDICINAL: Crushed dried leaves mixed with water are
used at childbirth and to treat stomach ailments. The plant
is also used as a snuff for nasal problems.

CEREMONIAL: Hoary ground-daisy is used by the singer
in the Water Way and as a medicine in the Night Chant and
other ceremonies.

REFERENCES

Elmore, Francis, *Ethnobotany of the Navajo,* 89.
Hocking, George M., "Some Plant Materials Used
Medicinally and Otherwise by the Navaho Indians in
the Chaco Canyon, New Mexico," *El Palacio,* 156.
Vestal, Paul A., *Ethnobotany of the Ramah Navajo,* 97.
Wyman, Leland, and Stuart Harris, *Ethnobotany of the
Kayenta Navajo,* 50, 62.
———, *Navajo Indian Medical Ethnobotany,* 20, 31, 48.

VERVAIN *(Verbena)*
spike verbena, Macdougal verbena

Verbena macdougalii Heller (verr-'bee-nuh
  mac-dew-'gull-eye)
Verbena: From the Latin *verbenae,* sacred boughs of olive
  or myrtle, used by the Romans.
macdougalii: Named for Dr. David Trembly Macdougal
  (1865–1958), of the Carnegie Institute,
  plant physiologist, and an authority on
  desert vegetation

NAVAJO NAME: *Tádídíín dootł'izh nitsaaígíí,* "large blue
  pollen"

DESCRIPTION & DISTRIBUTION
Spike verbena is an erect herb branching toward the top
into spikes of tiny, violet flowers. The main stem is squarish
and has pairs of hairy leaves that are somewhat wrinkly
above and toothed along their margins. Height may exceed 2 feet but not 3 feet. It is the tallest, most conspicuous
verbena on the reservation. Flowers June through
September.

In the ecotone (overlap) between the woodland of Colorado pinyon *(Pinus edulis)* and Utah juniper *(Juniperus
osteosperma)* and the forest of ponderosa pine *(Pinus
ponderosa)* and Gambel oak *(Quercus gambelii)* at about 7,000
feet, spike verbena is one of the common roadside wildflowers. Its range in elevation is from 6,500 to 8,000 feet.

NAVAJO USES
CEREMONIAL: *Tádídíín dootł'izh nitsaaígíí* is used for blue
pollen when larkspur *(Delphinium* sp.) petals and pollen are
not available. The blue petals are dried, crushed, and used
ceremonially like corn pollen.

It is a Water Way, Life Way, and Plume Way medicine.

REFERENCES
Elmore, Francis, *Ethnobotany of the Navajo,* 72.
Vestal, Paul A., *Ethnobotany of the Ramah Navajo,* 41.
Wyman, Leland, and Stuart Harris, *Navajo Indian Medical
  Ethnobotany,* 32, 45, 71.

VIRGINIA CREEPER *(Parthenocissus)*
Virginia creeper

Parthenocissus vitacea: (Kern.) Hitchc.
    (parr-theh-noh-'siss-suss vye-'tay-see-uh)
Parthenocissus: From the Greek *parthenon,* "virgin," and
    kissos, "ivy" or "vine"
vitacea: Vine or grapelike

NAVAJO NAME: *Bit'ąą' ashdla'ii,* "five leaf one"

DESCRIPTION & DISTRIBUTION
Virginia creeper is a climbing woody vine with stems up
to 10 feet long, compound leaves of several leaflets, and
small, greenish flowers. Young stems are brownish but turn
gray-brown with age. Grasping tendrils secure the plant
as it clambers over bushes and rocks. Small blue-black berries ripen in the fall. Flowers May through September.

    Boulder-strewn stream shores and canyon-wall crevices
between elevations of 3,800 and 7,000 feet are suitable sites
for Virginia creeper in association with its relative, canyon
grape *(Vitis arizonica),* and with other shrubs.

NAVAJO USES
MEDICINAL: Swellings of an arm or leg are treated with a
lotion made of Virginia creeper leaves and berries soaked
in warm water.

    OTHER: If vines grow close by, they are often used to
cover summer houses (open structures made of slender
poles designed to keep the sun out and to let breezes in).
The berries are edible although they are said not to taste
very good.

    CEREMONIAL: *Bit'ąą' ashdla'ii* is used as a medicine in the
Mountain Chant.

REFERENCES
Personal communications, April 1980.

131

WHEATGRASS *(Agropyron)*
western wheatgrass, bluestem wheatgrass

Agropyron smithii Rydb. (ag-ro-'pi-ron smith-'eye)
Agropyron: From the Greek *agros,* "field," and *pyros,* "wheat"
smithii: Named for Jared Gage Smith, botanist, who worked for the United States Department of Agriculture in the late 1800s

NAVAJO NAME: *Tl'oh nitl'izí,* "brittle grass"

DESCRIPTION & DISTRIBUTION
Western wheatgrass is a pale gray or blue-green bunch-grass, although it has the underground rhizomes (stems) characteristic of many sodgrasses. It grows as tall as 2 feet but often is only about 1½ feet. Leaves are as long as 7 inches. It resembles other wheatgrasses (*Agropyron* sp.), the wild ryes (*Elymus* sp.), and the ryegrasses (*Lolium* sp.). Flowers inconspicuously April through June.

On good soil, usually of medium texture, it grows in patches or occasionally in extensive stands between elevations of about 4,000 and 8,000 feet in shrubland, woodland, and forest.

NAVAJO USES
CEREMONIAL: *Tl'oh nitl'izí* is burned as incense in the Enemy Way and other ceremonies.

REFERENCES
Franciscan Fathers, *An Ethnologic Dictionary of the Navajo Language,* 190.
Vestal, Paul A., *Ethnobotany of the Ramah Navajo,* 15.
Young, Stella, *Native Plants Used by the Navajo,* 110.

WILD BUCKWHEAT *(Eriogonum)*
redroot wild buckwheat, redroot eriogonum

Eriogonum racemosum Nutt. (ehr-ee-'og-on-um
    ra-seh-'moh-sum)
Eriogonum: "Woolly knee," for woolly stems and leaf
        bases of some species
racemosum: Bearing flowers in a raceme (elongated
        cluster)

NAVAJO NAME: *Łe'étsoh yiljaa'í*, "like a rat's ear"

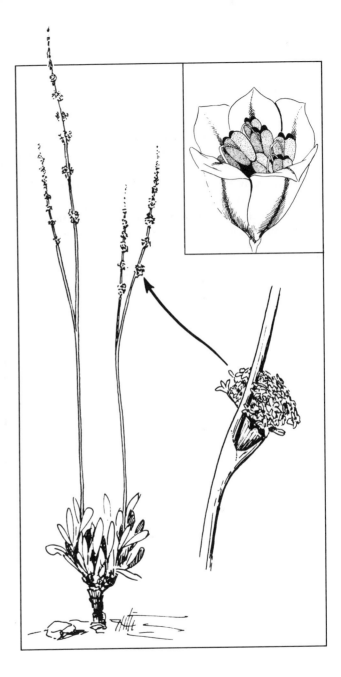

DESCRIPTION & DISTRIBUTION
Redroot wild buckwheat is a perennial herb with leafless,
flowering stems growing up to 2 feet tall from a woody
root crown. Leaves are basal (growing from the root crown
rather than from the stems). Whitish to pinkish flowers
bloom July through September.

    Between elevations of about 6,000 and 8,500 feet,
redroot wild buckwheat grows in communities of
Colorado pinyon *(Pinus edulis)* and Utah juniper *(Juniperus
osteosperma);* of big sagebrush *(Artemisia tridentata)* and
fourwing saltbush *(Atriplex canescens);* and of ponderosa
pine *(Pinus ponderosa)* and Gambel oak *(Quercus gambelii),*
on coarse and medium soils.

NAVAJO USES
MEDICINAL: Redroot wild buckwheat is used for a variety
of internal injuries: blood poisoning, backache, sideache,
venereal disease, and undefined internal injuries. The
medicine is made by soaking the whole plant in water; the
resulting liquid is drunk, or, for venereal disease, used as
a lotion for sores. Occasionally alum root *(Heuchera
parvifolia)* is added to the medicine for blood poisoning.
Łe'étsoh yiljaa'í is one of the ingredients of life medicine (see
yarrow).

    CEREMONIAL: *Łe'étsoh yiljaa'í* is an ingredient in the
medicine used in the Beauty Way and Life Way ceremonies.

133

HOUSEHOLD: Redroot wild buckwheat is edible; the leaves and stems can be eaten raw.

REFERENCES

Elmore, Francis, *Ethnobotany of the Navajo,* 42.

Franciscan Fathers, *An Ethnologic Dictionary of the Navajo Language,* 196.

Matthews, Washington, "Navajo Names for Plants," *The American Naturalist,* 775.

Vestal, Paul A., *Ethnobotany of the Ramah Navajo,* 23.

Wyman, Leland, and Stuart Harris, *Navajo Indian Medical Ethnobotany,* 19, 61.

WILLOW *(Salix)*
coyote willow, sandbar willow

Salix exigua Nutt. ('say-liks eks-ih-'jew-uh)
Salix: Classic name for willow; the name probably comes from the Celtic *sal,* "near," and *lis,* "water"
exigua: Small, little

NAVAJO NAME: *K'ai' łibáhígíí,* "gray willow"

DESCRIPTION & DISTRIBUTION

Coyote willow is a branching, open shrub occasionally attaining a height of about 10 feet but usually shorter. New twigs are yellowish to tan and somewhat fuzzy; as they age they become brownish and then grayish; old bark is gray. New leaves are also slightly hairy and appear drab. Pendulous clusters of female flowers produce fruits that rupture and release tiny seeds that are borne aloft by their hair whenever the wind blows in late spring.

Thickets of coyote willow stabilize sandy shores of washes, streams, and water impoundments up to elevations of about 7,000 feet in communities of Fremont cottonwood *(Populus fremontii),* Russian olive *(Elaeagnus angustifolia),* tamarisk *(Tamarix chinensis),* Goodding willow *(Salix gooddingii),* and red willow *(Salix laevigata).*

NAVAJO USES

MEDICINAL: The leaves of coyote willow are soaked in water, and the liquid is used as an emetic.

CEREMONIAL: *K'ai' łibáhígíí* is used in the Lightning Way and Big Star Way as a medicine and tobacco. It is also used for ceremonial equipment in the Lightning Way.

OTHER: Coyote willow is used for firewood when foods are to be cooked in ashes, because the ashes retain heat. For instance, a sheep's head, a Navajo delicacy, is cooked by placing the head, wrapped in a paper sack or aluminum foil, in a pit preheated by a willow fire. The head is covered with

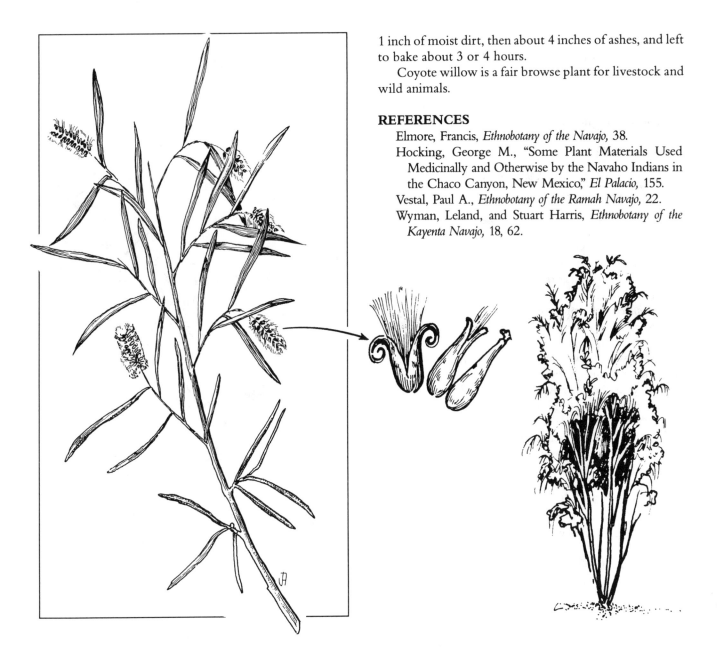

1 inch of moist dirt, then about 4 inches of ashes, and left to bake about 3 or 4 hours.

Coyote willow is a fair browse plant for livestock and wild animals.

REFERENCES

Elmore, Francis, *Ethnobotany of the Navajo*, 38.

Hocking, George M., "Some Plant Materials Used Medicinally and Otherwise by the Navaho Indians in the Chaco Canyon, New Mexico," *El Palacio*, 155.

Vestal, Paul A., *Ethnobotany of the Ramah Navajo*, 22.

Wyman, Leland, and Stuart Harris, *Ethnobotany of the Kayenta Navajo*, 18, 62.

WOLFBERRY *(Lycium)*
desert wolfberry, rabbit thorn, box thorn, matrimony vine, tomatillo

Lycium pallidum Miers (ly-'see-um 'pal-lid-um)
Lycium: Ancient Greek name for a prickly medicinal
plant, which grew in Turkey
pallidum: Pale

NAVAJO NAME: *Haashch'éé'dą́ą́,* "god's food"

DESCRIPTION & DISTRIBUTION

Desert wolfberry is a rounded, thorny, branchy, deciduous shrub shorter than 5 feet. Upper twigs change from gray-green to gray-white (appearing quite whitish in winter) as they age; older stem bases are gray. Flowers are greenish white. Fruits are purplish to orangish. A very similar and closely related shrub is Anderson wolfberry *(Lycium andersonii),* somewhat smaller with yellow-white flowers, narrower leaves, and bright orange fruits. Flowers late April through early June.

Desert wolfberry is found between 4,500 and 6,800 feet. It intermingles and possibly hybridizes with Anderson wolfberry; neither, however, is very abundant. Associates are goldenweeds *(Aplopappus* sp.), rabbitbrushes *(Chrysothamnus* sp.), and saltbushes *(Atriplex* sp.). Occupied sites are localized and scattered within the range—often mounds of coarse soil over ancient ruins or more recent buried rubble or cobblestones.

NAVAJO USES

MEDICINAL: The ground root is used for toothache. The bark and dried berries are part of Navajo life medicine (see yarrow).

CEREMONIAL: *Haashch'éé'dą́ą́'* is used in the Evil Way and Female Shooting Way for equipment and for a ceremonial emetic.

OTHER: The red berries of desert wolfberry are eaten raw or cooked. As they have an astringent quality, they are usually cooked or ground with an equal quantity of white food clay (mineral substance found on the reservation and mixed with native foods to take away the bitterness).

REFERENCES

Elmore, Francis, *Ethnobotany of the Navajo*, 74.
Hocking, George M., "Some Plant Material Used Medicinally and Otherwise by the Navaho Indians in the Chaco Canyon, New Mexico," *El Palacio*, 153.
Matthews, Washington, "Navajo Names for Plants," *The American Naturalist*, 775.
Steggerda, Morris and R. B. Eckardt, "Navajo Foods and Their Preparation," *American Dietetic Association Journal*, 222.
Vestal, Paul A., *Ethnobotany of the Ramah Navajo*, 42.
Wyman, Leland, and Stuart Harris, *Ethnobotany of the Kayenta Navajo*, 41.
——— , *Navajo Indian Medical Ethnobotany*, 27, 45.
Young, Stella, *Native Plants Used by the Navajo*, 20.

YARROW *(Achillea)*
western yarrow, common milfoil

Achillea millefolium L. (ak-il-'lee-uh mill-lih-'foh-lih-um)
Achillea: Named for Achilles, the hero of Homer's *Iliad*, who is credited with discovering the medical uses of this genus. Another Achilles, a pupil of Chrion, is also given this credit.
millefolium: Mille, "thousand"; *folium,* "leaves"

NAVAJO NAME: *Hazéíyiltsee'í,* "chipmunk-like tail"

DESCRIPTION & DISTRIBUTION
Western yarrow is a perennial herb growing from an underground stem that also bears the roots. The erect above-ground stem is usually unbranched, has very finely divided leaves, and is topped with a cluster of medium-sized, white flowers; the height is about 2 feet. Leaves resemble those of a carrot but are quite fuzzy. The fruit is hard and dry like the sunflower seed. Flowering occurs late June through late September.

Common in mountain communities of ponderosa pine *(Pinus ponderosa)* and Gambel oak *(Quercus gambelii),* and of Colorado blue spruce *(Picea pungens)* and Douglas fir *(Pseudotsuga menziesii),* it is also scattered in moist places below the forests. The range in elevation is from about 5,000 feet upward to 8,000 feet. Among its close associates in the forest are geraniums *(Geranium* sp.), Kentucky bluegrass *(Poa pratensis),* and bracken fern *(Pteridium aquilinum);* lower, in groves along washes, Rocky Mountain beeplant *(Cleome serrulata),* pigweeds *(Amaranthus* sp.), common cocklebur *(Xanthium strumarium),* and Texas doveweed *(Croton texensis)* may be found nearby.

NAVAJO USES
MEDICINAL: *Achillea millefolium* is one of a large group of plants known as "medicine twigs," *azee' tsiin,* or Navajo life medicine.

Unlike other Navajo herbal medicines that must be picked just before use, these are gathered, dried, and saved until needed, or are taken on trips for emergencies. The plants are ground before use, mixed with water, and drunk or rubbed on the skin. Four life medicines can be used in an emergency but it is better to have six or more mixed together.

Yarrow is used alone for fever and headaches. To relieve headaches caused by sore eyes, this plant is added to the fire and the smoke directed at the eyes. Yarrow is used for healing sores on people and animals. It is especially good for healing saddle sores on horses.

CEREMONIAL: *Hazéíyiltsee'í* is used in Mountaintop Way, Night Way, and Enemy Way. It is made into a fumigant and a medicine in the Mountaintop Way, and a medicine in the Enemy Way. In addition, the plants are burned, and the ashes applied as "blackening" in the Enemy Way. A lotion made of the crushed plant mixed with water is used to treat eye irritations caused by wearing Night Way masks.

REFERENCES

Elmore, Francis, *Ethnobotany of the Navajo,* 79–80.
Franciscan Fathers, *An Ethnologic Dictionary of the Navajo Language,* 114–15, 186, 371–72, 409.
Matthews, Washington, "Navajo Names for Plants," *The American Naturalist,* 773.
Vestal, Paul A., *Ethnobotany of the Ramah Navajo,* 47.
Wyman, Leland, and Stuart Harris, *Ethnobotany of the Kayenta Navajo,* 44, 61.
——— , *Navajo Indian Medical Ethnobotany,* 27, 46, 74.
Young, Stella, *Native Plants Used by the Navajo,* 100.

APPENDIX

(Page numbers of plant discussions appear in parenthesis)

Light Brown Dye Recipe

1 lb. common mountain mahogany (68) rootbark
½ lb. thinleaf alder (4) bark
1 cup juniper (55) ash water
1 lb. yarn

Fill a 5-gallon can half-full of water. Add bark and boil for 1 hour. Strain. Add juniper ash water and boil 15 minutes. Add wet yarn to the dye. Stir and boil for 1 or 2 hours. Rinse thoroughly.

Navajo Native Weed Seed Bread★

2 ears ripe Indian corn
¾ cup beeplant (12) seeds
½ tsp. salt
Enough boiling water to make a soft dough

Finely grind corn and seeds. Add salt and enough boiling water to make a soft dough. Shape dough into 4 × 2-inch cakes (should make approximately 15). Bake in hot ashes.

Hoop and Pole Game

This game was played on a 10-foot-wide and 15-yard-long, east-west strip of bare, level ground. The play consisted of the winner of each previous roll, rolling the hoop first to the east, then to the west. As the hoop rolled, the players tried to throw a pole so that the hoop would land on top of it. Points were awarded for the way the hoop rested on the buckskin thongs decorating the pole — two strips tied horizontally on a vertical strip. They were referred to as turkey tracks because the center thong was always the longest. The hoop was made of yucca and covered with buckskin or twine, and the pole was made of birch (16).

★*This recipe, in which any edible wild weed seed can be substituted, was developed by Navajo students in a home economics class at Fort Wingate Vocational High School, Fort Wingate, New Mexico.*

Gold Dye Recipe★

2 lbs. fresh cliffrose (27) twigs and leaves
¼ cup raw alum (aluminum sulfate—found at the base of
  some rock cliffs on the reservation)
1 lb. yarn

Boil twigs and leaves in 5 gallons of water for 2 hours. Strain, add raw alum, then boil 10 minutes. Add wet yarn, stir again. Boil 2 hours. Allow wool to remain in dye bath overnight. Rinse.

★*Developed by Mrs. Stella Young at Fort Wingate Vocational High School, Fort Wingate, New Mexico.*

Games Using Dice Made of Cottonwood (29)

Seven small two-sided dice, about 1 × 2½ inches, are used in *Da'aka' tsosts'id,* or Seven Cards. Bystanders bet as the dice are tossed and caught in a Navajo basket. Scoring varies, but points are awarded by the colors showing when the dice land. Six of the dice are black on one side and white on the other. The seventh is black on one side and red on the other.

Longer cottonwood dice were used in the Women's Stick Game, *Tsidil.* The legendary Navajo female gambler, *Nihwiilbiihii,* invented *Tsidil* and then was challenged to a game by the Pueblo Gambler, as the story goes, when the Pueblo Gambler had the assistance of Eastwind, who gently blew the white sides of the dice up. Because of that, Navajos are said to be exceptionally good at *Tsidil.*

Tsidil is played with forty stones set in a circle. Bets are made before the game starts by placing money under a stone in the center. Each of the five or six players picks a twig or stick for a marker to move around the circle. Players move their markers according to how the three cottonwood dice (1 × 4 inches, black on one side, white on the other) land when they are tossed to the stone in the center. Moves are made according to the following point schedule: two black and one white, 3; all black, 5; all white, 10. All white gets another turn. If a marker lands on the spot taken by another player, the first one on the spot must return to the beginning. The first player around the circle wins.

Nutritional Composition of Goosefoot, or Common Lambsquarters

Lambsquarters (43) is one of the few native foods on the Navajo Reservation whose nutritional composition is known. A one-hundred-gram serving of lambsquarters, cooked and raw, has the following composition:

	Water %	Calories	Protein g	Fat g	Carbohydrates g	Fiber g
Raw	84.3	43	4.2	0.8	7.3	2.1
Boiled/Drained	88.9	32	3.2	0.7	5.0	1.8

	Ascorbic Acid mg	Calcium mg	Iron mg	Thiamine mg	Riboflavin mg	Niacin mg	Vit. A IU
Raw	80	309	1.2	.16	.44	1.2	11,600
Boiled/Drained	37	258	0.7	.1	.26	0.9	9,700

The seeds have not been analyzed.

Adistsiin Ritual

The bride takes the wedding *adistsiin* to her new home for good luck. Prayers are said each time the sticks are used to stir mush, sunwise, right to left. Afterwards, the sticks are cleaned and held up while a prayer is said:

May it be cool; may it be warm;
May I acquire property;
May my neighbors and I have good health;
May my neighbors feel friendly toward me.

The *adistsiin* are made by gathering an odd number of greasewood (46) sticks in the spring. The sticks are placed in coals to remove thorns and loosen the bark. Next, the bark is removed and the sticks are cut the same length, about 2 feet long. The bundle of sticks is tied at intervals so that the sticks will dry straight. The ends nearest the root are sharpened. When the sticks are dry, they are tied together in the middle. Only the pointed ends are used to stir food.

Juniper Ash Water (*Juniperus osteosperma*, 55)

Gather reddish branches. Set them on fire while holding them over a skillet to catch the ashes. Only the needles should burn. Add boiling water to one cup of ashes. Stir and strain through a food brush.

Navajo Blue Corn Bread Recipe

Boil 3½ cups water. Add 1 cup strained ash water and 6 cups blue cornmeal. Knead until dough is soft and firm. Shape into 2 or 3 loaves. Bake in hot ashes for 1 hour. Remove ashes and quickly wash off. Serve warm.

Today, Navajo blue corn bread is frequently cooked like a thick pancake on a griddle on top of the stove.

Juniper Wool and Buckskin Dye Recipe

Soak juniper leaves and twigs in water. Boil for about 1 hour. Strain. Add a small amount of alum (aluminum sulfate—found at the base of many rock cliffs on the reservation) and simmer until it is dissolved. Add wet yarn when dye has cooled. Let simmer 1 hour, then soak until desired color is obtained. Rinse wool until water is clear. Dry.

Rose Taupe Dye Recipe

1 lb. mountain mahogany (68) rootbark
1 lb. prickly-pear (75) fruit
1 lb. yarn
1 cup juniper ash water (recipe p. 141)

Boil rootbark for 1 hour in a 5-gallon can of water. Strain and cool until lukewarm. Soak cactus fruit in 1 quart of lukewarm water and strain, pushing pulp through strainer. Add pulp and water to rootbark solution. Add yarn, which has been in juniper ash water. Allow to ferment in a warm place for 1 week. Rub dye into yarn often. Rinse thoroughly.

Reddish Brown, or Henna, Dye Recipe

¼ lb. mountain mahogany (68) rootbark
½ lb. Navajo tea (*Thelesperma gracile*)
½ lb. raw alum (aluminum sulfate—found at the base of many rock cliffs on the reservation)
1 lb. yarn

Boil bark and tea in 5 gallons of water for 2 hours. Strain, add alum, and stir well. Boil 10 minutes. Add wet yarn and stir well. Boil 2 hours. Allow yarn to ferment in the dye bath in a warm place for 1 week. Rub yarn often. Rinse thoroughly.

Traditional Navajo Bow

The traditional bow was made of a 4-foot branch of oak (72) stripped of its bark, flattened on the lower side, and smoothed and rounded on the upper edge. It was heated over a fire until it could be bent into shape. Both ends were pressed into a reverse curve so that the finished bow would have a slightly serpentine appearance.

Sheep fat was rubbed into the wood, and the bow set in the sun or near the fire for several days to allow the grease to penetrate the wood and dry. The bow center and ends were wound with sinew or the back was covered with several layers of glued sinew before being coated with boiled horses hoofs. This made the bow elastic.

A red paint, made from the red leaf or bark galls of the oak mixed with red clay or pinyon (*Pinus* sp.) gum, was used to paint red stripes on arrows. Black stripes were sometimes added.

Nutritional Content of Prickly Pear (76) Fruit
(100 grams of raw fruit)

Water %	Calories	Protein g	Fiber g	Carbohydrates g	Ash g	Calcium mg	Phosphorus mg
88	42	.5	10.9	1.6	.5	20	28

Iron mg	Sodium mg	Potassium mg	Vit. A IU	Thiamine mg	Riboflavin mg	Niacin mg	Ascorbic Acid mg
.3	2	166	60	.01	.03	.4	22

Nutritional Content of Pinyon (78) Seeds

	Water %	Calories	Protein g	Fat g	Carbohydrates g
unshelled	3.1	1,671	34.2	159.2	53.9
shelled	3.1	180	3.7	17.2	5.8

	Calcium mg	Phosphorus mg	Iron mg	Vit. A IU	Thiamin mg
unshelled	32	1,589	13.7	80	3.37
shelled	3	171	1.5	10	.36

	Riboflavin mg	Niacin mg	Ascorbic Acid mg
unshelled	.61	11.8	trace
shelled	.07	1.3	trace

The Ponderosa Cradleboard

The cradleboard is described in detail in the oral Navajo creation stories. The one illustrated here is the style in use today. A cradleboard made traditionally, as the proper prayers are said, helps insure the good health of the infant.

A solid piece of wood is cut, bottom up, from the east side of a young ponderosa pine (80) that grows in a remote area and is unlikely to be cut down. The grain of the wood must remain in the direction it grew. The cradleboard may be made any size. The wood is cut with a saw using another cradleboard as a pattern. The top ends of the cradleboard are pointed if the board is for a girl, flattened when it is for a boy. Holes for buckskin lacings are bored with a hot wire, then the board is sanded smooth with a stone. The cradleboard is stained with a mixture of red ocher and tallow.

Before disposable diapers were available, the cradleboard was lined with shredded bark of juniper or cliffrose. The bark could be cleaned and dried in the sun, then reused.

The baby is laced into the cradleboard from the top down. An outgrown cradleboard may be used as a toy or may be saved for another child of either sex.

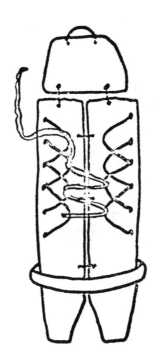

Nutritional Content of Purslane (86)

(100 grams of leaves and stems)

	Calories	Protein g	Fat g	Carbohydrates g	Fiber g	Calcium mg	Phosphorus mg
raw	21	1.7	.4	3.8	.9	103	39
cooked & drained	15	1.2	.3	2.8	.8	86	24

	Vit. A IU	Thiamine mg	Riboflavin mg	Niacin mg	Ascorbic Acid mg	Iron mg
raw	2,500	.03	.1	.5	25	3.5
cooked & drained	2,100	.02	.06	.4	12	1.2

143

Yellow Wool and Basket Dye Recipe

Boil the flowering tops of rubber rabbitbrush (87) for 6 hours. Separately, heat alum (aluminum sulfate — found at the base of many rock cliffs on the reservation) until it becomes soft. Add to wool and boil until the desired color is reached, then boil 2 more times.

Roasted Corn Recipe

A pit equal to the volume of corn to be roasted is dug. (A pit 5½ feet deep — 5 feet wide at the bottom, narrowing to 20 inches in diameter at the top — is reported to have been used to cook two wagonloads of corn.) Build a fire in the pit for as long as a day or until the surrounding soil is thoroughly heated. Lift the fire out with shovels and put the unhusked corn in the pit. Place a layer of spiny saltbush (108) on top of the corn and cover with hot dirt. Build a fire over the pit and leave to burn all night.

Nutritional Content of Sunflower (124) Seeds

(100 grams of hulled seeds)

Calories	Protein g	Fat g	Carbohydrates g	Fiber g	Ash g	Calcium mg	Phosphorus mg
560	24	47.3	19.9	3.8	4	120	837

Iron mg	Sodium mg	Potassium mg	Vit. A IU	Thiamine mg	Riboflavin mg	Niacin mg	Ascorbic Acid mg
7.1	30	920	50	1.96	.23	5.4	34

ANNOTATED BIBLIOGRAPHY

Bailey, Flora. "Navajo Foods and Cooking Methods." *American Anthropologist* 42(1940): 270–90. Recipes from Navajo women for many corn dishes and foods made from wild plants.

Bingham, Sam and Janet. *Navajo Farming,* Chinle, Arizona: Rock Point Community School, 1979. An excellent book and a must for anyone who wants to better understand Navajo culture. It contains planting information, stories, legends, games, and scientific information about farming on the Navajo Reservation.

Carpenter, Thorne M., and Morris Steggerda. "The Food of the Present-day Navajo Indians of New Mexico and Arizona." *The Journal of Nutrition* 18 (July–December 1939): 297–306. Laboratory analysis of Navajo foods.

Darby, William, et al. "A Study of the Dietary Background and Nutriture of the Navajo Indians." *The Journal of Nutrition* 60 (November 1956): Supplement 2.

Dodge, Natt. *100 Desert Wildflowers in Natural Color.* Globe, Arizona: Southwest Parks and Monuments Association, 1963.

——— . *100 Flowers of the Southwest Deserts.* Globe, Arizona: Southwest Parks and Monuments Association, 1969.

——— . *100 Roadside Wildflowers of the Southwest Uplands.* Globe, Arizona: Southwest Parks and Monuments Association, 1967. These related publications from Southwest Parks and Monuments are essential for a beginning botanist. They are easy to use and the brief but informative paragraphs give the beginner a feeling for the plant that makes recognition easier.

Elmore, Francis H. *Ethnobotany of the Navajo.* Albuquerque, New Mexico: The School of American Research, 1943. A seven-year study (begun in 1936) of the plants used by the Navajo in the Chaco Canyon area. Elmore purposely skipped over medicinal information (although some medical uses are included) because he knew other researchers in the area were working on medical uses of native plants. See Hocking.

——— . *Shrubs and Trees of the Southwest Uplands.* Globe, Arizona: Southwest Parks and Monuments Association, 1976. The best guide to shrubs and trees of the reservation area. Scientific and ethnic information mixed with an easy-to-use format, plus the best pronunciation and translation guide of scientific names readily available today.

Franciscan Fathers. *An Ethnologic Dictionary of the Navajo Language.* St. Michaels, Arizona: St. Michaels Press, 1910. A painstaking study of the Navajo; one of the most complete and detailed accounts of the Navajo daily and ceremonial life at the turn of the century.

Hocking, George M. "Some Plant Materials Used Medicinally and Otherwise by the Navaho Indians in the Chaco Canyon, New Mexico." *El Palacio* 63(1956): 146–65. The plants studied were collected near Pueblo Bonito in the Chaco Canyon National Monument in 1942–43. Dr. Hocking began work on the materials in 1950 and the paper was presented to the American Association for the Advancement of Science meeting in December 1955 in Atlanta, Georgia.

James, George Wharton. *The Indians of the Painted Desert Region.* Boston, Massachusetts: Little, Brown and Company, 1904. A travelog typical of its time. Surprisingly, James identifies plants by their scientific names.

Kavasch, Barrie. *Native Harvests, Recipes and Botanicals of the American Indian.* New York: Vintage Books, 1979. A beautiful book with outstanding recipes and illustrations. The book's sales support the American Indian Archaeological Institute and continue its education and ethnobotany endowment. The only flaw from a Navajo viewpoint is an untraditional Navajo Fry Bread recipe, but the book is basically recipes of eastern Indians.

Kearney, Thomas H., and Robert H. Peebles. *Arizona Flora.* Berkeley, California: University of California Press, 1960. A descriptive listing of 3,438 species of flowering plants, ferns, and fern allies growing uncultivated in Arizona. An Arizona botanist's basic book.

Kirk, Ruth F. "Navajo Bill of Fare." *New Mexico Magazine* 16(June 1941): 6. Text and pictures of Navajo foods.

Kluckhohn, Clyde, and Dorothea Leighton. *The Navajo.* Cambridge, Massachusetts: Harvard University Press, 1946. The authority, the book everyone tells you to read although now, after 40 years, is of more historical than practical value.

Kluckhohn, Clyde, W. W. Hill and, Lucy Wales Kluckhohn, et al. *Navajo Material Culture.* Cambridge, Massachusetts: Harvard University Press, 1968. A how-to book including pictures, drawings, and explicit information on how the Navajos made household and ceremonial items.

Kreig, Margaret B. *Green Medicine, the Search for Plants That Heal.* Chicago, Illinois: Rand McNally and Company, 1964. The stories behind the discoveries of folk medicines that led to quinine, digitalis, curare, birth control pills, cancer medications, and other plant-derived medicines. A good bibliography is included for those who want to learn more about pharmacognosy.

Locke, Raymond Friday. *The Book of the Navajo.* Los Angeles, California: Mankind Publishing Company, 1976. A Navajo history, beginning with the Navajo origin myths and continuing into present day society. Its one serious flaw: no footnotes or bibliography. Otherwise, an excellent book.

Lehr, J. Harry. *A Catalogue of the Flora of Arizona.* Phoenix, Arizona: Desert Botanical Garden, 1978. An update to *Arizona Flora,* this book is a current checklist of Arizona's flora in a handy field-guide size.

Martin, Niels. *Common Range Plants, Navajo Reservation, A Preliminary List.* Tucson, Arizona: Cooperative Extension Service, University of Arizona, March 1973. An English/Navajo/scientific listing of common range plants by a university extension agent living in Tuba City.

Martin, Dr. William C. and Charles R. Hutchins. *Flora of New Mexico in Two Volumes,* Forestburgh, NY: Lubrecht & Cramer, 1980. The new standard.

McDougall, W. *Seed Plants of Northern Arizona.* Flagstaff, Arizona: Northern Arizona Society of Science and Art, Inc., 1973. Complete descriptions of reservation plants (all five northern Arizona counties are included) designed to make plant identification precise. Follows the same format as *Arizona Flora* but is somewhat easier to read. Botanists in Northern Arizona use McDougall as the standard.

Matthews, Washington. "Navajo Names for Plants." *The American Naturalist* 20, no. 9 (September 1886): 767–77. Dr. Matthews, an army physician, was assigned to Ft. Wingate, New Mexico, in 1880, 16 years after the Navajos had been released from the prison camp at Bosque Redondo. He spent 4 years with the Navajo learning about their arts, medicines, and ceremonies as well as working as a physician. In 1884, he was transferred to Washington, D.C., as curator of the Army Medical Museum. He had spent 21 years among Indian tribes in a dozen states, but his writings of the Navajo are his most acclaimed works.

Mindeleff, Cosmos. "The Navajo Reservation." *The Indian Advocate* 12, no. 11 (1901): 319–24, and 13, no. 8 (1901): 225–31. An interesting early look at the Navajo.

Niethammer, Carolyn. *American Indian Food and Lore: 150 Authentic Recipes.* New York: Collier Books, 1974. Well-researched, detailed information on how to gather and prepare wild foods, with additional ethnic uses and other facts about each plant. Excellent drawings.

Steggerda, Morris, and R. B. Eckardt. "Navajo Foods and Their Preparation." *American Dietetic Association Journal* 17 (March 1941): 217–25. First-hand recipes for preparation and presentation of Navajo native foods, animal and vegetable.

Stephen, A. M. "The Navajo." *American Anthropologist* VI (October 1893): 345–62. A comprehensive look at the Navajo lifestyle in the late 1800s.

Sweet, Murial. *Common Edible and Useful Plants of the West.* Healdsburg, California: Naturegraph Company, 1962. Scientific and ethnic information on 116 plants, with line illustrations.

Tschopik, Harry Jr. *Navajo Pottery Making.* Cambridge, Massachusetts: Harvard University, Peabody Museum of American Archaeology and Ethnography, 17, no. 1 (1941). A thorough study of Navajo pottery.

Vestal, Paul A. *Ethnobotany of the Ramah Navajo.* Reports of the Ramah Project, Papers of the Peabody Museum of American Archaeology 11, no. 4 (1952). Peabody Museum, Cambridge, Massachusetts. One of the few studies available on this somewhat separate community of Navajos.

Watt, Bernice K., and Annable L. Merrill, et al. *Composition of Foods, Agricultural Handbook No. 8.* Washington, D.C.: USDA, 1975. An analysis of 2,500 raw, processed, and prepared food items with adequate explanations of all tables. A valuable resource for anyone who is concerned with what they eat.

Wooten E. O., and P. C. Stanley. *Flora of New Mexico, Contributions from the U.S. National Herbarium* 19, Washington, D.C.: Smithsonian Institute, 1915. The first authorative document.

Wyman, Leland C., and Stuart K. Harris. *Navajo Indian Medical Ethnobotany.* Albuquerque, New Mexico: The University of New Mexico Bulletin III (1941): 1–76. Over 1,200 plants used for medicine — most were collected in the Pinedale, Coolidge, Smithlake, Chinle, and Ramah areas of the Navajo Reservation. The field work was done from 1933 to 1938.

———. *The Ethnobotany of the Kayenta Navajo.* Albuquerque, New Mexico: University of New Mexico Press, 1951. An analysis of the John and Louisa Wetherill ethnobotanical collection. Wyman and Harris had already published their *Navajo Indian Medical Ethnobotany* and were the logical choices of the Wetherill Memorial Fund to edit the notes of Louisa and John Wetherill. The Wetherills were traders who lived in southern Utah and later Kayenta, Arizona, from 1910 until their deaths in the 1940s. (See *Traders to the Navajo*, Francis Gillmor and Louisa Wade Wetherill, New York, New York, 1934.)

Young, Stella. *Native Plants Used by the Navajo.* United States Department of Interior, Office of Indian Affairs, March 1938, mimeograph. Mrs. Young was director of the home economics department at Ft. Wingate Vocational High School, Ft. Wingate, New Mexico, where this information was collected. Her specimens were identified by Dr. E. F. Castetter, of the University of New Mexico.

Young, Stella, and N. G. Bryan. *Navajo Native Dyes, Their Preparation and Use.* United States Office of Indian Affairs, Education Division, Indian Handcrafts, no. 2. n.d. Easy to follow natural dye instructions.

COMMON NAME INDEX

SCIENTIFIC NAME INDEX

AUTHORS & ILLUSTRATORS

VERNON O. MAYES came to the Navajo Reservation in 1958 from a ranch in southern California. He studied agriculture and range science at the University of California, agriculture and forestry at Utah State University, and biology and anthropology at Northern Arizona University.

BARBARA BAYLESS LACY developed the Navajo Health Authority Ethnobotany Project. A journalist (BJ University of Missouri), she lived on the Navajo Reservation from 1971 to 1980, and is now a writer living in Paradise Valley, Arizona.

JACK AHASTEEN, Navajo, was born and raised on the Navajo Reservation. He is an artist, political cartoonist, and illustrator whose work is seen in many local publications and art galleries.

JASON CHEE, Navajo, has lived on and off the Navajo Reservation. He has worked in all areas of commercial art, from mechanical and technical illustration to graphic design.